SMALL-SCALE ENTREPRENEURSHIP

SMALL-SCALE ENTREPRENEURSHIP

By
Dr. M. LAKSHMI NARASAIAH
M.A., Ph.D.,
Professor and Head,
Department of Economics,
Sri Krishnadevaraya University Post-graduate Centre,
Kurnool—518002 (A.P.)

DISCOVERY PUBLISHING HOUSE
NEW DELHI—110 002

First Published-2001
Reprint : 2012
ISBN 81-7141-582-2

© Author

Published by
DISCOVERY PUBLISHING HOUSE
4831/24, Ansari Road, Prahlad Street,
Darya Ganj, New Delhi-110002 (India)
Phone: 3279245 • Fax: 91-11-3253475

Printed at:
Dynamic Printers

Preface

The concept, Small-Scale Industry covers a wide range of activities; and its definition changed from time to time. The latest definition (1990) of Small-scale Industries is quite broad-based. The investment ceiling in plant and machinery for small-scale industries is Rs. 60 lakhs and for ancillary units, it is Rs. 75 lakhs.

The role of village and small-scale industries in the development of national economy has been stressed by the Government of India in its Industrial Policy Resolution of 1956 and, in the successive Five Year Plan documents. The main advantage of small-scale industries is that they provide large scale employment at relatively smaller capital cost. Small industries are expected to meet a substantial part of the increased demand for consumer goods and simple producers' goods. They facilitate mobilisation of resources and skill, which might otherwise remain unutilised. They offer a method of ensuring more equitable distribution of national income.

The main policy of the Government of India for the development programmes for small-scale industries has been to remove the hurdles and the factors causing of industrial sickness.

Absence of suitable factory accommodation has been one of the major problems of small industries in India. A large number of small-scale industries are spread all over the country concentrating mostly in towns. These industries are generally situated in congested areas with no space for expansion. This is because of non-availability of infrastructure facilities like raw material, power, water, transportation, banks, post offices, machinery, trained artisans and markets for finished goods in semi-urban and rural areas in India.

Author

Contents

1

Introduction

STATEMENT OF THE PROBLEM

The Small Scale Industry has been recognised as one of the most appropriate means of developing the industrial economy of backward countries. Small Scale industries facilitate the tapping of resources which otherwise would remain unused. These resources included entrepreneurship, capital, labour and raw materials. They can mobilize rural savings which may otherwise remain idle or may be spent on luxuries or channelled into non productive ventures.

They are fairly labour intensive, Small Scale Industries which create employment opportunities at a relatively low capital cost. In India, there is a basic problem of absorbing the surplus manpower in non-agricultural jobs and providing additional employment opportunities for the growing population.

Small Scale Industries contribute significantly to the strengthening of the industrial structure. Small Scale Industries serve as seed-beds of entrepreneurship. They serve the developing economy not only by their output of goods but also by functioning as a nursery of entrepreneurial and managerial talent. This role of Small Scale Industries is of decisive importance in any economy.

Such industries lead to the creation of employment opportunities as a dispersed basis not only in large cities and towns but also in smaller towns and far-flung regions. The establishment of Small Scale Industries would therefore made it possible to reverse the current trend of the migration of the people from rural to urban areas.

The development of Small Scale Sector has been importance in India because the Small Scale Unit requires less capital outlay and at the same time, it provides more employment than the large scale sector. A Small Scale Unit does not require highly sophisticated technology. It can therefore, be useful in backward areas where the people have yet to be trained to meet the challenge of sophisticated technology.

Soon after independence our national leaders recognised the role of Small Scale Sector in the development of the economy of India and laid a solid foundation for its accelerated development through active policy support and creation of an institutional frame work. The Industrial Policy Resolutions of the Government of India, from 1948 to 1991 visualised integrated growth of both the large and Small Scale Sectors and recognised the social and economic contribution of Small Scale Sector. These Industrial Policy Resolutions states that the Government of India would stress the role of cottage and village and Small Scale Industries in the development of the national economy. The policy further envisaged that the decentralised sector should acquire sufficient vitality to be self supporting and its development be integrated with that of the large Scale Industry.

Anantapur district is located in the southern part of Andhra Pradesh. It is an economically backward district. The main livelihood of the people is agriculture. For the past several decades, there has been failure of rains in this region. As there is no prospects of agriculture in this district, people have stated move to neighbouring districts, particularly to Karnataka areas to ekeout their livelihood.

In view of this prevailing situation, the unemployed educated youths are evincing interest to establish Small Scale Industries with the help and assistance of Scheduled Banks, State Finance Corporations etc. The Government of Andhra Pradesh has initiated several industrial programmes to make the State on par with other industrially developed states. As a part of its policy, the Government of Andhra Pradesh has announced several incentives to entrepreneurs who want to start Small Scale Industrial units. The establishment of Small Scale Industrial units is best suited to this district in view of the availability of raw materials from agriculture and mineral based and other industries. The establishment of Small Scale Industries will be a boon to the people of Anantapur District to lift the people above poverty line. The Small Scale Industries, inspite of encouraging entrepreneurs, generates employment opportunities to the needy. The pivotal role of District Industries centre in advising the enthusiastic entrepreneurs to move forward to achieve their goal is highly commendable.

The burning problem facing the Government is how to solve employment. As we know, the Government alone cannot start or declare war against unemployment, the unemployed educated youths should take positive interest in establishing Small Scale Industries in support of the Governmental efforts, to solve this unemployment problem.

For establishing Small Scale Industries, the know how of capital structure, employment generation, locating the industrial belt and other aspects of industrial establishment are a must for any prospective entrepreneurs. There seems to be no other go except establishing Small Scale Industries where ever feasible to solve the problem of Unemployment. Such an attempt would necessarily provide the opportunity for the optimum utilisation of local resources to serve the local needs.

The Large Scale Industry is urban based. It has resulted in the neglect of agriculture and industry in the Rural areas. The establishment of Small Scale Industries can serve as an effective means of reducing the prevailing imbalances. It helps in accelerating process of overall development of the State.

Select Review of Literature

Some studies have been undertaken on various programmes and incentives to small industries promotional activities of DICS and problems associated with the implementation of the promotional institutions and the problems faced by the entrepreneurs. SIET (1972)[1] in its study on Hire-purchase has observed that the growth in the number of units and the expansion of capital intensity alone may not create the necessary impetus to the growth unless considerable productivity changes have also been effected through fuller capacity utilisation. Most of the units utilising full-capacity have been either big export-oriented industries or local-need-based activities. The reasons for this under utilisation were mostly insufficient demand for inadequate financial resources for working capital. In a study a spatial diversification of manufacturing industries in Uttar Pradesh, Papola (1979)[2], while furnishing evidence of a continued spatial concentration has noted a decline in the share of factory employment in five most industrialised districts from 57 per cent in 1960 to 55 per cent in 1975 and also in 10 industrially least developed areas from 1.10 per cent to 0.56 per cent. He has concluded that there is a need for a small degree of dispersal of manufacturing activity in favour of backward areas with some degree of industrialisation. Malgawakar (1973)[3]. In his study of problems of small industry in Andhra Pradesh has found the lack of infrastructure as a general problem. The industrial estates alone cannot overcome the locational disadvantages. The infrastructural facilities were either very weak or non-existent in rural areas. In Urban areas, with necessary industrial climate and infrastructural facilities, the growth of industries was relatively faster. The scarcity of indigenous raw materials has been a serious bottleneck. Scarce raw materials supplied through quotas were not sufficient to meet the demands of the units. There were delays in the disbursement of loans due to the existence of procedural delays and insistance of tangible securities.

The development of Small Industry also depends on the size of market which in turn depends partly on the efficiency of the size of market which in turn depends partly on the efficiency of the distribution of machinery. It is observed that there was a time lag between sales and realisation of sale proceeds and this affected production of the enterprise. This study has also found that the incentives provided by the state and the centre were not within the reach of all the entrepreneurs in rural areas.

Andhra Pradesh Industrial Technical Consultancy Organisation (A.P.I.T.C.O) and Kerala Industrial Technical Consultancy Organisation (K.I.T.C.O.) 1980[4] conducted a study of the various problems faced by the industries in three states viz., Kerala, Karnataka and Andhra Pradesh. The study revealed that the serious problem faced by the units was the inadequacy of working capital. 69 per cent of units in Kerala, 44 per cent of units in Karnataka and 52 per cent of units in Andhra Pradesh were facing the same problem. The next serious problem was marketing as 30 per cent of the units in Kerala felt it as another setback. Non-availability of raw materials has affected the productivity of several units in all the states especially, in industry groups such as metal-products in Kerala, Chemicals, Rubber and Plastics and metal products in Karnataka, machinery and parts, metal products and chemicals in Andhra Pradesh. It was observed, that the delay in getting timely finance also hampered the productivity of the units and this led to high cost of production, as observed in a few cases, in all the states.

Sarma (1982)[5] who made a study on growth and problems of Small Scale Sector in Andhra Pradesh, has observed that the backward districts of the State improved their relative positions in terms of units employment and capital during 1966-75. Majority of the small units are confronted with the problems of raw materials and finance.

Sekhar (1983)[6] in his study has observed that the location policies were successful in narrowing the disparities of industrial location in different states. The value added and employment were more equally distributed among the states during 1960 and 1975 as measured by the Theils' inequality and the Harschman Hirfindhal's indices. He also examined intra-regional distribution of industry by comparing the degree of concentration of industrial employment in 1961 and 1971 by grouping cities by size and arrived at the conclusion that, for India as a whole, the degree of concentration of employment in household industry has declined substantially between 1961 and 1971. However, the non-household industry maintained its level of concentration during the period.

Rajula Devi (1984)[7] in her study made on the evaluation of Rural Industries Project Programme found the following serious deficiencies (i) Some part of the assistance was provided to relatively larger amongst small scale units, (ii) Assistance was diverted to towns which were excluded from the purview of the scheme (iii) Rural artisans did not receive adequate credit. Indian Institute of Management (1988)[8] in its study conducted on "Evaluation of DIC programme in Andhra Pradesh observed that the General Manager, DIC, as Secretary to the single window committee is expected to hasten up the processing of entrepreneurial cases and thus help the minimisation of delay. Single Window Committee just recommends and requests for speeder action and the DIC have no powers to hasten up and clear up such delayed cases. Several entrepreneurs in every DIC have been annoyed to find their cases long pending with developmental agencies and local bodies due to indifferent attitude and lack of emphathetic understanding of entrepreneurial problems. With regard to the activities like term-loan assistance, working capital assistance, capital subsidy, land and factory shed, many entrepreneurs seemed to have received the requisite help from DIC. In these activities, DICs have mostly recommending powers. For raw materials and other information, DIC's seem to be playing a very small role.

DICs have been functioning for over a decade since their inception. The above studies have tried to indicate certain deficiencies of various schemes including District Industries centres but they have not evaluated the performance of DIC at a regional level. Hence, it is time to undertake an evaluative study which is area-specific since India is a vast country with varied socio economic conditions.

Bhagavati Committee[9] opposes fast introduction of mechanisation designed to replace human labour but, at the same time, recommends introduction of sophisticated technology in certain areas. The Committee recommends reduction to the maximum extent possible in the installed capacity in various industries in order to generate employment in the industrial field. The committee virtually favours creation of employment at any cost without going into the economics of the scheme.

In a study on rural industrialisation in India Bepin Behari[10] examined the problems, possibilities and perspectives of rural industrialisation and discussed the crisis in Indian villages and the need for the new strategy of rural industrialisation and the provision of fuller employment in rural and small scale industries and technologies. He traced out agricultural development encouragement to village and small scale industries and general awareness for incorporating appropriate technologies as principal sources of impetus to the programme of technological transformation in rural India. Further he reviewed various measures taken by the Government towards rural industrialisation, local industrial growth, agro-based industries, mini-rural cement plants, utilisation of annual waste and harnessing of natural power.

K.V. Bhanujam[11], has suggested that appropriate technology should be developed to promote the rural small industries, N.V. Ratnam[12] opines that infrastructure development for industrialisation in the rural areas and investment in basic services designed to realise the full potential of the human resources in the rural areas should receive a high priority.

Gunnar Myrdal[13] has recommended the adoption of a strategy based on predominantly labour intensive techniques for creating capital and production. The line of approach has been followed up by Sen[14] Johnson[15], Vinod Vyasulu[16] and Raj Krishna[17] suggesting the need for the adoption of an employment oriented strategy of industrialisation to absorb the rural labour force.

Tin Bergen[18] opines that the strategy of industrialisation should lay emphasis on labour intensive industries which will create more employment and maximise income. He suggests the adoption of labour-intensive but reasonably efficient techniques. Gautam Mathur[19] opines that the appropriate techniques in the consumption goods sector will be of a low degree of mechanisation creating incidentally a lot of employment per unit of investment of scarce capital. Dr. Wu, Jageh[20] in his study pointed out that both the capital output ratio and wage-capital ratio show an inverse relationship with capital intensity. He recommends the setting up of SSI in countries having large unemployment. A.C. Minocha[21] has suggested that the strategy of employment-oriented industrialisation should aim at the development of SSI in rural areas. K.M. Rastogi[22], in his study suggests that the SSI should make use of the indigenous resources in an optimal manner. UNIDO's[23] study indicates that the small enterprises with low-level of investment per worker tend to achieve a higher productivity of capital.

The Committee[24] on the villages and SSI in its report has stressed that the setting up of SSI will provide employment to the people ir rural areas.

K.M. Rastogi[25] has also made a case study of Madhya Pradesh which he calls a unique case of growing unemployment and poverty amidst plenty. He is in favour of only Small Scale and Village Industries which make optimum use of indigenuos resources and techniques. According to him, there are hundreds of items which can be produced in rural and Small Scale Industrial units more economically than in a large sector.

Bhagavati[26] Committee opposes fast introduction of mechanisation designed to replace human labour but, at the same time recommends introduction of sophisticated technology in certain select areas. The Committee recommends reduction to the maximum extent possible in the installed-capacity in various industries in order to generate employment in the industrial field. The Committee virtually favour creation of employment at any cost without going into the economics of the scheme.

The Present Study

In a vast country like India with varied resource base and socio economic conditions, macro level studies may not throw much light as the problems of all regions thus more micro level studies for each region are necessary for understanding the prospects and problems of small scale industrial units in different regions of our country. The present study conducted in Kurnool District, one of the drought prone and backward districts of Andhra Pradesh is a modest attempt in this direction, which throws much light on the problems and prospects of small scale industrial units at the district level.

OBJECTIVES OF THE STUDY

The objectives of the present study are:

1. To study the growth and performance of small-scale industries in Kurnool District.
2. To examine the problems of small-scale industries in Kurnool District.

HYPOTHESIS

There is a significant growth in small-scale industry in Kurnool district.

METHODOLOGY

Data Base

Survey method has been adopted for this study, Data for the study have been collected from both primary and secondary sources. Secondary sources include Census Reports, Plan Documents of Central and State Governments, Financial Institutions, District Industries Centre and Statistical Abstracts of India and Andhra Pradesh. Primary data have been collected from sample small-scale industrial units through a schedule constructed for the purpose.

Tools of Analysis

In addition to usual statistical measures such as ratios, percentages and averages, analyses are employed at appropriate contexts in the study. And also various statistical tools are used in the study to analyse the data as follows:

REFERENCES

1. Small Industries Extension Training (SIET). A Study of National Small Industries corporation is Hire-purchase Scheme. Hyderabad SIET Institute, March, 1972.

2. *Papola, T.S.*, Spatial Diversification of Manufacturing Industries in Uttar Pradesh, Lucknow, Giri Institute of Development Studies, 1979.

3. *Malgawakar, P.D.*, "Problems of Small Industry. A Study in Andhra Pradesh", Hyderabad, SIET, 1973.

4. *Andhra Pradesh Industrial Technical Consultancy Organisation and Kerala Industrial Technical Consultancy Organisation,* "Survey of Industrial Estates in India, Semion Industrial Development of Backward Areas, sponsored by Industrial Development Bank of India, May 7, 1980.

5. *Sarma, R.K.*, Industrial Development of Andhra Pradesh. A Regional Analysis, Bombay, Himalaya Publishing House, 1982.

6. *Sekhar, A.*, Uday, Industrial Location Policy—The Indian Experience, World Bank Staff working paper No. 620, Washington, 1983.

7. *Devi Rajula,* "Industrialisation Holds Key to Rural Development Kurukshetra, December, 1984, p. 34.

8. *Indian Institute of Management*, Evaluation of DIC Programme Andhra Pradesh, Bangalore, May, 1988.

9. *Government of India*, Report of the Committee on Unemployment (Bhagavati Committee, New Delhi) (1973).

10. *Bepin Behari*, Rural Industrialisation in India, Vikas Publishing House, New Delhi (1976).

11. *Banujam, K.V.,* (1964), Poverty Alleviation through Rural Industrialisation, Kurukshetra (India's Journal of Rural Development) Vol. XXXIII No. 1 October, (1984) pp. 51-53.

12. *Rathnam, N.V.;* (1984). Rural Industrialisation and IRDP Kurukshetra (India's Journal of Rural Development) Vol. XXXIII No. 3, December, (1984) pp. 4-8.

13. *Myrdal Gunnar*, Asian Drama, An Enquiry into the Poverty of Nations, The Penguin Press, London, (1968).

14. *Sen, A.K.*, Employment, Technology and Development, Oxford. (1975).

15. *Johnson Harry*, G., Technology and Economic Interdependence. (1975).

16. *Vyasulu Vinod*, (1976). Technology and Change in Underdeveloped Societies, Economics and Political Weekly, August, 28 (1975).

17. *Raj Krishna*, Rural Unemployment Policies for the Fifth Plan, Economic and Political Weekly, March, 3, (1973).

18. *Tin Bergen*, J. Discussion in Manar Hada (Ed) Problems of Unemployment in India, Allied Publishers, p. 7.

19. *Mathur, Gautam*, True Employment and Non-employment in D.L. Narayana et. al., (Eds), Planning for Employment, Sterling Publishers, (1980) pp. 1-9.

20. *Wu, Jageh*, Capital Intensity and Economic Growth in Under-developed Countries, Ising Hua Journal of Chinese Studies, New Series, III-IV (1968) pp. 219-245.

21. Minocha, A.C. Industrial Development in M.P. Regional Structure and Strategy for Employment Oriental Industrialisation in D.L. Narayana et. al., (Eds) O. Peit (1980) pp. 259-3077.

22. *Rastogi, K.M.*, Employment Generation through S.S.V. and C.I. A Case Study of M.P., in D.L., Narayana et. al., (Eds), op cit., pp. 308-320.

23. UNIDO SSI in Latin America, Publication No. 111337, (1969) p. 56.

24. *Government of India*, Planning Commission (1956). Report of the Committee on Village and SSI (Chairman, D.G. Karve).

25. *Rastogi, K.M.*, Employment Generation through S.S. Village and Cottage Industries, A Case Study of M.P. in D.L. Narayana et al., (Eds). (1980).

26. *Government of India*, Report of the Committee on Unemployment (Bhagavati Committee), New Delhi. (1973).

2

Small-scale Industries in India —Policies, Programmes and Performance

INTRODUCTION

Over the years, the Government of Developing countries have adopted positive measures to defeat the forces of stagnation. To perform this gigantic task, well-considered and most suited policy of economic development has been framed. The growth process of these countries aims at accelerating the economic development to enhance the social welfare. Infact, the economic change is a part of a wider social change and the economic development is a long-term process of intrinsic growth. Therefore, the task of policy making has a vital role to play in selecting the desired objectives and suitable alternatives for stimulating the economic growth. It also requires a careful examination of the existing institutional framework, social values, economic requirements and their implications, keeping in view, the need for rapid social and economic development of the economy.

Now-a-days, most of the developing countries are following the thesis that industrialisation is a process of growth and as such is organically linked both to the social and economic past and to the parallel processes of social and economic development.[1]

The thesis reaffirms the importance of industrialisation as an effective means for solving the problems of economic and social progress in developing countries of the world.

Since the end of the Second World War, most of the developing countries are giving top priority to industrialisation. Actually, the planners of most of the developing countries have regarded industrialisation as the panacea for underdevelopment and poverty. The most primitive economies are now keenly interested in rapidly enlarging manufacturing industry. It is in rapid industrialisation "in which they place a major hope of finding a solution to their problems of poverty, insecurity and over-population and ending their newly realised backwardness in the modern world.[2]

The poor countries believe that industrialisation brings some basic changes in the production-functions and techniques, occupational structure and the level of activities in the other sectors of the economy. These changes will remove the obstacles which were retrading the growth and will raise the standard of living. Gunnar Myrdal has rightly pointed out the relationship of industrialisation to economic development when he observes "the manufacturing industry represents, in a sense, a higher stage of production in advanced countries. The development of manufacturing has been concomitant with these countries, spectacular economic progress and rise in the levels of living. Not least in the underdeveloped countries, the productivity in industry tends to be considerably greater than in the traditional agricultural pursuits.

In the light of the aforesaid facts, it cannot be denied that industrialisation, in general, can be the best means of achieving the higher growth rate and raising the living standards of the people. In the context of the developing economies, a few a specific objects and policies of industrialisation have been generally agreed to by the planners. They are to provide work for growing populations, to raise the standard of living by increasing the per capita, net national income and often to improve balance of the payments situations."[3] Thus the development of small scale industries alone can provide large-scale employment to the growing population in developing countries.

Role of Small Scale Industries in Industrialisation of India

India is often described as an underdeveloped country. The term 'underdeveloped' implies that the resources human and material of the country have not been properly harnessed with the result that the people have to live in poverty. They are under fed and physically weak and their working capacity is low. 'Underdevelopment' implies that the level of real income and capital per head of population is low as judged by the standards in developed countries of North America and Western Europe. In under developed countries, there is no large-scale application of the fruits of scientific and technological advances to agriculture and industry. Subsistence production is generally important for the people, the markets are comparatively narrow and manufacturing industry is usually unimportant.[4]

In many developing countries, manpower is relatively abundant. It is, therefore, imperative that their full and effective utilisation should become a focal point of socio-economic policies. Emphasis has to be laid on small scale industries to absorb the surplus manpower in these countries.

The concept, small scale industry covers a wide range of activities and its definition changed from time to time. The latest definition (July, 1990) of small scale industries is quite broadbased. All industries with a capital investment of Rs. 20 lakhs in plant and machinery are classified as small scale industries. The smaller units with a capital investment of Rs. 2 lakhs in plant and machinery are classified as tiny units. Units with a capital investment in plant and machinery varying between Rs. 20 lakhs and Rs. 25 lakhs are classified as ancillary industries.

The development of small scale sector has been important in India because of the following reasons: First, the small scale unit requires less capital outlay and at the same time, it provides more employment than the large scale sector. Second, a small scale unit does not require highly sophisticated technology. It can, therefore, be useful in backward areas where the people have yet to be trained to meet the challenge of sophisticated technology.

Importance of Small Scale Industries

Apart from their inherent usefulness in terms of numerical superiority, small scale industries play a vital role in the economic growth of developing countries as discussed below:

(i) Utilisation of Resources

Small Scale Industries facilitate the tapping of resources which otherwise would remain unused. These resources include entrepreneurship, capital labour and raw materials. They can mobilize rural savings which may otherwise remain idle or may be spent on luxuries or channelled into non-productive ventures.

(ii) Employment Generation

Since they are fairly labour-intensive small scale industries create employment opportunities at a relatively low-capital cost. In India, there is basic problem of absorbing the surplus manpower in non-agricultural jobs and providing additional employment opportunities for the growing population.

(iii) Generation of Foreign Exchange

Small Scale Industries facilitate substantial foreign exchange savings and earnings. A wide range of consumer and simple produced goods, now being imported, can be economically produced domestically on a small scale basis as long as adequate facilities are provided.

(iv) Diversification of Industrial Structures

Small Scale Industries contribute significantly to the strengthening of the industrial structure. Many more articles can be produced economically by the small scale than that of large scale industries.

(v) Entrepreneurial Development

Small Scale Industries serve as seedbeds of entrepreneurship. They serve the developing economy not only by their output of goods but also by functioning as a nursery of entrepreneurial and managerial talent. This role of Small Scale Industries is of decisive importance in any economy where the industrial structure consists of a few large scale and medium sized ones, on the one hand, and of large numbers of traditional industries such as artisan units, handicrafts and cottage industries on the other.

(vi) Regional Development and Industrial Dispersal

The concentration of industrial and other activities has given birth to the phenomenon of the so called pockets of development where economic and social change is achieved at much faster rate than in the outlying rural districts.

This trend, although predominant, can be checked and corrected through the establishment of small scale industries. For one thing, such industries lead to the creation of employment opportunities on a dispersed basis not only in large cities and towns but also in smaller towns and far flung regions. The establishment of small scale industries would, therefore, make it possible to reverse the current trends of the migration of the people from rural to urban areas.

Small Scale Industry and Industrial Policy Resolution

A study of the industrial policy documents reveals that small scale industrial unit has been assigned an important role throughout the period since Indian political independence. Thus, for example protection and promotion of small scale industry has all along been listed as a major objective in all of the industrial policy documents. The policy statements also indicate the lines on which the Government has been taking or contemplating concrete steps.

The point may be highlighted by referring to the Industrial Policy resolutions.

Industrial Policy Resolution, 1948

This policy Resolution (1948) recognized the fact that cottage and small scale industries have a very important role in the national economy, offering as they do give scope for individual, village or co-operative enterprise and means for the rehabilitation of displaced persons, These industries are particularly suited for the better utilisation of local resources and for the achievement of local self sufficiency in respect of certain types of essential consumer goods like food, cloth and agricultural implements. The healthy expansion of cottage and small scale industries depend upon a number of factors like the provision of raw materials, cheap power, technical advice, organised marketing of their produce, and where necessary, safeguard against the intensive competition by large-scale manufacture, as well as on the education of the workers in the use of the best available technique.

Industrial Resolution, 1956

This Resolution Policy of the Government of India 1956 stressed the role of cottage, village and small scale industries in the development of the National economy. In relation to some of the problems that need urgent solutions, offer some distinct advantages. They provide immediate large scale employment. They offer a method of ensuring a more equitable distribution of the national income and facilitate an effective mobilisation of resources of capital and skill which might otherwise remain unutilised.

Some of the problems that unplanned urbanisation tend to create will be avoided by the establishment of small centers of industrial production all over the country.

The Government of India has been following a policy of supporting cottage and small scale industries by restricting the volume of production in the large scale sector, by differential taxation or by direct subsidies. While such measures will continue to be taken, whenever necessary, the aim of the State policy will be to ensure that the decentralised sector acquired sufficient to be self supporting its development integrated with that of large scale industry.

Industrial Policy Resolution, 1977

The importance assigned to small scale industry is emphasised in still greater measure in the 1977 Industrial Policy Resolution.

The emphasis of Industrial Policy before the adoption of Industrial Policy Resolution was mainly on large industries neglecting cottage industries completely giving minor role to small scale industries. The firm policy of the Government was to change this approach. The main aim of the new industrial policy was the effective promotion of cottage and small scale industries widely dispersed in rural areas and small towns.

From the greater emphasis laid on the small scale industry by 1977 Resolution, big push has been given to the growth of the decentralised sector. Thus, for example the list of industries reserved for this sector has been expanded to cover 504 items from the earlier list of 180 items (since then the list has been further expanded to cover in all over 807 items). The statement also declared the intention of the Government to provide maximum support to the small scale industries for product standarisation quality control, marketing etc., on priority basis. Within the small scale sector a sub sector of tiny units has been created and this sub sector was expected to receive preferential treatment even within small scale sector.

It was also proposed in the statement to enact special legislation for protecting the interest of cottage and household industries. Each district to have one agency called the "District Industries Centre" to deal with the requirements of this industry. A separate wing to be created in the Industrial Development Bank of India for Small Scale Industries to provide effective financial support to this sector. Finally, special efforts use envisaged for modernising khadi and village industries and for promoting appropriate technologies all around.

Industrial Policy Resolution, 1980

The Industrial Policy statement made by Government of India on 23rd July, 1980 primarily sought to harmonise the growth in the small scale sector with that in the large and medium sectors. The emphasis in the new policy was on fostering the complementarity between the large and small sectors so that the new dichotomises (which are more apparent than real) between the two sectors did not distort the economic pattern.

The broad socio-economic objectives of the New Industrial Policy of 1980 were set out as follows:[5]

i) Optimum utilisation of installed capacity

ii) Maximising production and achieving higher productivity

iii) Higher employment generation

iv) Correction of regional imbalances through a preferential development of industrially backward areas

v) Strengthening of the agricultural base by according a preferential treatment to agrobased industries and promoting optimum inter-sectoral relationship

vi) Faster promotion of export oriented and import substitution industries

vii) Promoting economic federalism with an equitable spread of investment and the dispersal of returns amongst widely spread small but growth units in rural as well as urban areas.

viii) Consumer protection against high prices and bad quality.

An important element of the new policy was the raising of the investment limits of the tiny and small scale sectors. These limits were redefined in terms of investment in plant and machinery and were fixed at Rs. 2 lakhs for tiny sector instead of Rs. 1 lakh Rs. 20 lakhs for the small scale sector instead of Rs. 10 lakhs and Rs. 25 lakhs instead of Rs. 15 lakhs for ancillaries. This step was essentially a pragmatic one and took into account the significant price rise that occurred in the last five years following the fixation of the investment limits for the small scale sector.

This decision would it was hoped bring into the fold of the small scale sector, a number of technology oriented units whose growth would be backed by a suitable system of incentives. The new industrial policy spelt out some of these incentives which was proposed to be provided so that the small scale sector might grow in a significant measure and contribute to the national economy.

The policy statement of 1980 made it clear that the existing support programme for marketing as well as the reservation of items in the small scale sector would continue. The basic thrust of this policy was to ensure a continued growth of the small scale sector without at the same time, inhibting the growth of other sectors. In this context, automatic growth for a large number of industries in the medium and large sector would be ensured so that they could grow without hindrance.

A special emphasis was laid on the establishment of 'nucleus plants' in backward districts around which a programme of ancillarisation would be developed. To quote from the statement: "The proposed nucleus plants in industrially backward district would generate a net work of small scale units, or the existing network of small scale units in an area would acquire a faster growth by the coming up of a nucleus plant in the area. In between the nucleus large plants and the satellite ancillaries, the Government would permit a system of linkages for an integrated industrial development.[6] The new policy targets set for the sixth plan viz., production of the value of more than Rs. 35, 000 crores, employment of 11 million persons and with promotion of exports totalling nearly Rs. 2,000 crores. The small scale sector might look forward to a steady and balanced growth within the frame work of the new policy statement of the Government of India.

INDUSTRIAL POLICY (1990)

The Government has been considering the need to take measures for promotion of small scale and agro based industries and to change procedures for grant of industrial approvals.

Main Objectives

2. In pursuance of Industrial policy to re-orient industrial growth to serve the objective of employment generation, dispersal of industry in rural areas and to enhance the contribution of small scale industries to exports, it has been decided to take the measure enumerated below.

Investment Ceiling for Small Scale and Ancillary Units

3. The investment ceiling in plant and machinery for small scale industries (fixed in 1985) would be raised from the present Rs. 35 lakhs to Rs. 60 lakhs and correspondingly, for ancillary units, from Rs. 45 lakhs to Rs. 75 lakhs. In order to enable small scale industries to play an important role in the total export effort, the small scale units which undertake to export at least 30% of the annual production by the third year will be permitted to step up their investment in plant and machinery to Rs. 75 lakhs.

Tiny Units

4. Investment ceiling in respect of tiny units would also be increased from the present Rs. 2 lakhs to Rs. 5 lakhs. However, with regard to their locations, the population limit of 50,000 as per 1981 census would continue to apply. Steps will be taken to ensure better in flow

of credit and other vital inputs and to improve infrastructural support to the constituents of the tiny sector.

Reservation Items

5. Presently, 836 items have been reserved for exclusive manufacture in the small scale sector. Efforts be made to identify more items amenable to similar reservation. Encroachment and violation by large scale units into areas, reserved for small scale sector will be effectively dealth with.

Central Investment Subsidy

6. A new scheme of Central Investment subsidy exclusively for the small scale sector in rural and backward areas capable of generating higher level of employment at lower capital cost would be implemented.

Upgradation of Technology

7. With a view to improving the competitiveness of the products manufactured in the small scale sector, programmes for modernisation and upgradation of technology would be implemented. A number of technology centres, tool rooms, process and product development centres, testing centres, etc., will be set up under the umbrella of an apex technology development centre in the Small Industries Development Organisation (SIDO).

Flow of Credit

8. To ensure adequate and timely flow of credit for small scale industries, a new apex bank known as Small Industries Development Bank of India (SIDBI) has already been established. One of the major tasks of SIDBI and other commercial banks/financial institutions would be to channelise need-based, higher flow of credit, both by way of term loan and working capital, to the tiny and rural industries. A targeted approach will be adopted to ensure implementation and to facilitate monitoring this objective.

Review of Fiscal Concessions

9. The existing regime of fiscal concessions will be reviewed, both to provide sustained support to the units in the small scale sector and to remove the disincentives for their graduation and further growth.

Identification of Locations

10. An exercise will be undertaken to identify locations in rural areas endowed with adequate power supply and intensive campaign will be launched to attract suitable entrepreneurs, to provide all other inputs and foster small scale and tiny industries. Similarly, industries which are not energy intensive will be identified for proliferation in rural areas where power supply is presently a constraint.
11. In order to widen the entrepreneurial base, the Government would lay particular emphasis on training a women and youths under the entrepreneurial development programme. A special cell would be established in Small Industries Development Organisation (SIDO) and state directorates of industries to assist women entrepreneurs.

Relaxation in Bureaucratic Controls

12. One of the persistent complaints of the small scale units is their being subjected to a large number of acts/laws, being required to maintain a number of registeres, submitsplethora of returns and face an army of inspectors, particularly in the field of labour legislations. These bureaucratic controls will be reduced so that unnecessary interference is eliminated. Further procedures will be simplified and paper work cut down.

Expansion in Activities of KVIC and KVI Board

13. In order to assist the large number of artisans engaged in rural and cottage industries, activities of the Khadi and Village Industries Commission (KVIC) and KVI board will be expanded and these organisation will be strengthened to discharge the responsibility more effectively. Special marketing organisations at the Central and State levels shall be created to assist rural artisans in marketing their products

and also in supply of raw materials. Besides providing concessional credit, training facilities and free consultancy to groups of artisans will also be provided.

Agro Processing Industries

14. In agro processing industries, greater success has been achieved where growers and processors have been integrated, as in the case of sugar. For the success of other agro-based industries also, close links must be forged between the growers and processor units. Industrial policy will, therefore, especially promote projects which are organised in close co-operation the basis of joint ownership. Growers will be encouraged to set up processing units within the framework of co-operative societies or similar institutional frame work. This will also ensure the transmission of better technology for enhanced agricultural production.
15. In sectors where units require licensing, the policy will also encourage location of processing units in rural areas here growers are concentrated. Apart from economic benefits of proximity to raw materials it will help in dispersal of industry and increasing employment in rural areas.
16. Agro-processing industry will receive high priority in credit allocation from the financial institutions. In apportionment of working capital banks will give higher priority to such industries as compared to the rest of the industrial sector.
17. In order to bring the best technology available to these industries, technology approvals will be given within 30 days of presentation to the Secretariat for Industrial Approvals in the Department of Industrial Development. Government will actively promote and generate adoption of new technologies in the field.

Procedures for Industrial Approvals

18. Indian industry must be made more competitive internationally. It also needs to be released from unnecessary bureaucratic shackles by reducing the number of clearances required from the Government.

While the Government will continue to examine large projects in view of resource constraints, decisions in respect of medium sized investments will be left to the entrepreneurs. To achieve these objectives, the following decisions have been taken.

Delicensing

19. All new units up to an investment of Rs. 25 crores in fixed assets in non-backward areas and Rs. 75 crores in centrally notified backward areas will be exempt from requirement of obtaining licence/ registration.

Capital Goods (C.G.)

20. For the import of capital goods, the entrepreneur would have entitlement to import up to a landed value of 30 per cent of the total value of plant and machinary required for the unit.

Raw Materials and Components

21. For import of raw materials and components, imports will be permissible up to a landed value of 30 per cent of the ex-factory value of annual production. The ex-factory value of production will exclude the excise duty on the item of production. Raw materials and components on OGL will not be included within this 30 per cent limit. For all licensable items of raw materials and components, import licensing procedures will continue to operate.

Foreign Collaboration

22. In respect of transfer of technology, if import of technology is considered necessary by the entrepreneur, he can enter in to an agreement with the collaborator, without obtaining any clearance from the Government, provided that royalty payment does not exceed 5 per cent on domestic sales and 8 per cent of exports. If, however, lump-sum payment is involved in the import of technology, the proposal will require Government clearance, but a decision will be communicated to the entrepreneur within a period of 30 days.

Foreign Investment

23. Keeping in view the need to attract effective inflow of technology, investment up to 40 per cent of equity will be allowed on an automatic basis. In such proposals also, the landed value of imported C.G., shall not exceed 30 per cent of value of plant and machinery.

Minimum Economic Size

24. In order to ensure that investment leads to production of goods that attain international competitiveness and that maximum efficiency is ensured, the unit would have to confirm to the minimum economic size in cases where such a size has been prescribed.

Expansion

25. The de-regulation suggested above would cover all cases of expansion and would not be restricted only to new units.

Broad Banding

26. The existing Broad Banding Scheme would continue to be in force. In addition, if no extra investment is required, no clearance from the Government would be necessary for production and sale of any new item by existing units. This would not include those items which are reserved for small scale industries.

Location Policy and Environmental Clearance

27. The location policy would not be applied to such industries by the Centre except for location in and around metropolitan cities location will not be permissible within 20 Km. calculated from the periphery of the metropolitan area except in prior designated industrial areas and for non-polluting industries such as electronics, computer software and printing. It will be upto State Governments to regulate industrial locations keeping in mind local conditions and requirements and their respective spatial development plans and zoning and town planning laws. Similarly, environmental clearance would have to be obtained from the prescribed authority at the state level. In future, central

legislation should introduce new provisions, that law would automatically to these units as well.

Export Oriented Units

28. 100 per cent export oriented units (EOUs) and units to be set up in export processing zones (EPZs) are also being delicensed under the scheme up to an investment limit of Rs. 75 crores.

Convertibility Clause

29. Such investments shall be exempt from the "convertibility clause" applicable to financing by Indian Financial Institutions.
30. It may be clarified that in the application of the proposals for exemption 836 items which are reserved for production in the small scale sector will continue to be excluded.
31. The above proposals will be applicable to all manufacturing items in a specified list. The list shall follow the nomenclature of the Indian trade classification based on the harmonised system. In each section of the classification, apart from positive mention of approved items, those not permissible shall be specifically excluded from the benefit of the proposals listed above. Approval for excluded items will be as per the existing industrial policy regime and procedures.
32. Units set up by MRTP/FERA companies will be covered by the procedures set out above, but they will continue to need clearances under the provisions and regulations of these two acts.
33. The existing De-licensed Industries Scheme, Exempted Industries Scheme and BCTD Registration System will stand abolished.

Development of Small Scale Industries during Plan period

Till independence, only cottage industries, village industries, rural industries or agro-based industries were considered to be small industries. The National Planning Committee, set up in 1938 under the chairmanship of Pandit Jawaharlal Nehru, constituted a panel to study this problem. With the dawn of the planned era in the country, the Government has been following a policy of promotion as well as protection of the small industries sector but the protection would be gradually reduced as and when promotional activities began to produce results.

First Five Year Plan (1951-56)

In the First Five Year Plan, a major step taken for the development of village and small scale industries was the establishment of All India Boards to advise and assist in the formulation of the programme of development of small scale industries, including sericulture and coir. Although during the Second World War, small industries were set up throughout the country to meet the Defence requirements, a number of these disappeared totally or partially at the end of the war. The First Plan attempted to indicate some of the problems which were involved in formulation substantial development programmes for small industries and handicrafts and divided small industries into three groups viz., those which exist independently, those integrated with and those offering competition to, large scale industries, stores, purchase and replacement of imports were mentioned as the two directions in which the demand for products of small scale production, establishment of new township as in the river valley projects and training, research and finance these were the aspects stressed.[7]

Second Five Year Plan (1956-61)

The total outlay on small scale industries in the Second Five Year Plan was Rs. 180 crores as against Rs. 43 crores in the First Plan. A number of new programmes were organised and steps were taken to provide a more assured market for the products of some of the industries. Reservation of the production of certain varieties of cloth and certain types of agricultural implements, prohibition of further expansion in certain large-scale industries like vegetable oils, rice milling, leather foot wear, match etc., and the laying down of separate targets of production for the small scale and the large scale sectors of certain industries like bicycles sewing machines were some of the steps taken.

In the later period of the Second Plan, marketing conditions for the some of the small scale industries improved following the intensification of import restrictions. Programmes for village and small scale industries and problems connected with their implementation were reviewed by the Karve Committee on Village and Small Scale Industries (Second Five Year Plan) which was appointed by the Planning Commission in June, 1955. The programme Evaluation Organisation made a study of rural industries in selected community development blocks. In spite of shortages of certain basic raw materials many small industries notably machine tools, sewing machines, electric fans and motors, bicycles, builders hardware and hand tools expanded considerably at the rate of 25 per cent to 50 per cent per annum. The number of registered companies with authorised capital of less than Rs. 5 lakhs each and engaged inprocessing and manufacturing increased by 1,160 during 1957-1961. Sixty industrial estates were completed, and the programme for small scale industries as a whole provided full time employment to 3 lakh persons.[8]

THIRD FIVE YEAR PLAN (1961-1966)

The main objectives of the Third Five Year Plan in regard to the programme for village and small scale industries were:[9]

i) To improve the productivity of the workers and reduce production costs by placing a relatively greater emphasis on positive forms of assistance, such as improvement in skill, supply of technical advice, better equipment and credit

ii) To reduce progressively the role of subsidies, sales, rebates and sheltered markets

iii) To promote the growth of industries in rural areas and in small towns.

iv) To promote the development of small scale industries as ancillaries to large industries, and

v) To organise artisans and craftsman on co-operative lines.

In the Third Five Year Plan (1961-66) a total outlay of Rs. 264 crores was proposed for programmes of village and small industries, made up to

Rs. 141 crores for schemes of the States and Union Territories and Rs. 123 crores for the centre and centrally sponsored programmes and schemes. In addition, Rs. 273 crores were expected to be invested from private sources, including banking institutions and Rs. 20 crores on the programmes of community development, rehabilitation of displaced persons, social welfare and welfare of backward classes. Part-time and fuller employment was envisaged for 8 million persons, and additional full time employment for 6.3 lakh persons during the Third Plan.

Fourth Five Year Plan (1969-1974)

The Four Five Year Plan (1969-74) proposed a total outlay of Rs. 370 crores in the public sector for the development of village and small industries, exclusive of the outlays on the development of these industries in the programmes for community development, rehabilitation of displaced persons and development of special areas. About Rs. 400 crores were expected to be invested from private sources, including banking institutions. Thus, a total outlay of nearly Rs. 800 crores was expected to be available for small scale industries under the Fourth Plan.

The main programme during the Fourth Plan were to entrust the work of administration of credit facilities under the State Aid to Industries Act, training and common service facilities, quality marketing and consolidation of the Industrial Estates Programme, to the States, The Central Government continued to implement schemes related to industrial research, industrial extension services, supply of machines on hire purchase terms etc.[10]

Fifth Five Year Plan (1974-79)

A significantly large number of persons, dependent on traditional industries like handloom, sericulture, coir, khadi and village industries, living below the poverty line, live mostly concentrated in rural and backward areas, some of them belong to the backward classes. Therefore, the principal objectives of the programme for the development of different small industries in the Fifth Plan were to facilitate the attainment of some of the major tasks for the removal of poverty and inequality in the consumption standards of these persons through the creation of large scale opportunities for fuller and additional productive employment and improvement in their skills so as to raise their level of earnings. Further more, the programme was reoriented to set up the production of some of the beside and essential articles for the messes and of the products which have a larger potential for exports. Taking into account the shortcomings in the implementation of the programmes during the Fourth Plan Period and the recommendations of the Task Forces set up in connection with the formulation of the programmes for these industries, the broad strategy of the programmes was:[11]

1. To develop and promote entrepreneurship and provide a package of consultancy service so as to generate the maximum opportunities for employment, particularly self-employment
2. To facilitate a fuller utilisation of skills and equipment of the persons already engaged in different small industries
3. To progressively improve the production techniques of these industries so as to bring them to a viable level, and
4. To promote these industries in selected growth centres in semi urban and rural areas, including backward area.

Sixth Five Year Plan (1980-85)

The Sixth Five Year Plan marked a significant stage in the development of small scale industry.

The promotion of village and small scale industries was to continue to be an important element in the national development strategy because of its very favourable capital output ratio and high employment intensity. During the sixth five year plan, the programmes for the village and small industries sector were framed with the following objectives:[12]

i) improvement in the levels of production and earnings, particulalry in the earnings of artisans, by upgrading skills and technologies and producer oriented marketing
ii) creation of additional employment opportunities on a dispersed and decentralised basis
iii) Ensuring a significant contribution to growth in the manufacturing sector through, inter alia, a fuller utilisation of existing installed capacities
iv) the establishment of a wider entrepreneurial base by providing appropriate training and a package of incentives
v) creation of a viable structure of the village and small industries sector so as to progressively reduce the role of subsidies; and
vi) expand efforts in export promotion.

In the light of the above objectives, the policy support for the development programmes relating to village and small industries during the Sixth Five Year Plan was along the following lines:

i) integration of the promotional programme in the sector with other area development programmes, and the adoption of a cluster approach, particulalry for the traditional industries
ii) restructuring of the organisational base at the district level to make it more effective and result oriented
iii) development of appropriate technologies and skills, their effective extension and transmission
iv) increased availability of raw materials, including the creation of buffer stocks, particulars of critical raw materials
v) accelerated flow of institutional funds, specially in favour of artisans, village industries and tiny units, and the rationalisation of the interest rate structure
vi) organisation of producer-oriented marketing both within and outside the country
vii) selective reservation of items for exclusive production in the purchase from the cottage and small industries

viii) effective promotion of ancillaries

ix) strengthening and extension of the cooperative form of organisation, particulalry for the cottage and tiny units and

x) building up of a sound data base to facilitate proper policy formulation and evaluation.

As a major contributor to the planned growth of employment, the small scale sector was to receive a very high priority. The development effort would be mounted on many fronts. If necssary, certain products would be reserved for manufacture exclusively in the small scale sector and excise duty differentials will ensure that the products of the small scale sector are cheaper for the public than similar products manufactured by the small scale sector.

To ensure a co-ordinated growth and minimise the number of contact points, District Industries Centres were to be setup. The transfer of research and technology to this sector was given much greater impetus. As for credit, the possibility of extending the margin money scheme was considered. In the marketing of products, a major effort was mounted to remove the middleman and to provide, through the cooperative sector, a remunerative outlet for the products of cottage industries. Steps would be taken to enhance the provision for training, technical assistance and other facilities.

The outlay on village and small scale industries was stepped up from Rs. 533.03 crores in the Fifth Plan to Rs. 1,780-45 crores in the Sixth Plan. Production targets for this sector have also been stepped up from Rs. 33,150 crores to Rs. 49,233 crores. Moreover, this sector was expected to create additional employment of 90 lakhs, raising the total to 326 lakhs. Exports use expected to increase from Rs. 2,225 crores in 1979-80 to Rs. 3,685 crores. It was estimated that the total exports during the Sixth Plan would be of the order of about Rs. 15,500 crores.

The outlays for the development of small scale industries in the successive Five Year Plans are shown in the Table 2.1.

Table 2.1
Plan-wise Allocation for Village and Small Industries

S.No.	Plan	VSI	Outlay for Industry	Total Plan	USI as the percentage of industry outlay	USI is the percentage of total plan outlay
1.	First	42	97	1,960	43.30	2.1
2.	Second	187	1,125	4,672	16.62	4.0
3.	Third	341	1,967	8,577	12.25	2.8
4.	Forth	243	3,107	15,779	7.82	1.5
5.	Fifth	592	9,581	39,426	6.18	1.5
6.	Sixth	1,980	17,290	1,09,646	11.45	1.8
7.	Seventh	2,753	22,461	1,80,000	12.26	1.5

Source: 1. For First Plan to Sixth Plan 25 Years of KVIC commerce Vol. 144, No. 3692, pp. 3950.
2. For Seventh Plan, Government of India, Seventh Five Year Plan 1985-90, Planning Commission, New Delhi, Vol. II 1985 p. 10.4.

But its proportionate share in industrial and total planout lays has gone down from nearly 43 per cent and 2.1 per cent in the First Plan to 12.26 per cent and 1.5 per cent in the Seventh Plan respectively. The outlays in village and small industries sector have dwindled during the plan period.

Seventh Five Year Plan (1985-90)

Within the overall focus on food, work and productivity laid down in the Seventh Five Year Plan the village and small industries sector would contribute towards improving the economic and occupational profile of rural-semi urban and weaker sections of urban communities through promotion of village and small scale industrial activities.[14]

The implementation of the Seventh Plan started in 1985-86. On completion of half the term of the Plan, a mid-term appraisal was made and placed before the parliament on 22/23 March, 1988.

For promotion of rural industrialisation Khadi village industries centres reorganised and professionalised. Further specific steps were taken to diversify industries in rural areas to remove regional inbalances have resulted in about 43.5 per cent of all industrial licences granted to backward areas during the first two years.[15]

Researcher and development efforts were stepped up and the results there of were transferred to the field level agencies, providing for some of the welfare measures including housing-cum-workshed facilities and thrift fund scheme for the benefit of the artisan type of units had been considered. In this plan period, the government started extending the basic support in terms of functional assistance like marketing, ancillarisation, credit flow, supply of raw material and critical inputs, technology, training etc. The Seventh Plan envisaged discouraging the setting up of industries on or around urban agglomerations and package of incentives were provided to attract industries in backward regions. The implementing agencies did set up cells to monitor, evaluate and build an effective information service system so as to enable a periodic assessment of various promotional programmes.

PUBLIC SECTOR OUTLAYS AND PLAN PROVISIONS FOR VILLAGE AND SMALL INDUSTRIES

The public sector investment for fostering the village and small industries (VSI) during the plan era is shown in Table 2.1 absolute terms the investment, in village and small industries sector are increased from plan to plan.

Seventh Plan, Government of India, Seventh Five Year Plan 1985-90, New Delhi, 1985. It is noticed from the table the production has increased from Rs. 10.93 Crores to Rs. 807.06 crores. Employment from 3.02 lakh persons to 24.84 lakh persons, sales from Rs. 0.90 crores to Rs. 880-46 crores and earnings from Rs. 3.6 crores to Rs. 320 crores during First Plan to Seventh Plan period.

Table 2.2

Plan-wise production, Employment, Sales and Earnings in Village Industries

S.No	Plan	Production (Rs. in crores)	Employment (in Lakh persons)	Sales (Rs. in crores)	Earnings (Rs. in crores)
1.	First	10.93 (100.00)	3.02 (100.00)	0.90 (100.00)	3.60 (100.00)
2.	Second	33.16 (303.00)	5.64 (187.00)	28.36 (3151.00)	6.53 (181.00)
3.	Third	55.87 (511.00)	8.75 (290.00)	49.73 (5526.00)	10.74 (298.00)
4.	Fourth	122.00 (1116.00)	9.27 (307.00)	115.64 (12840.00)	22.15 (616.00)
5.	Fifth	347.98 (3184.00)	16.13 (534.00)	388.97 (43219.00)	78.84 (2190.00)
6.	Sixth	807.06 (7384.00)	24.84 (823.00)	880.46 (97829.00)	220.49 (6125.00)
7.	Seventh	1700.00 (15554.00)	30.00 (993.00)	1785.00 (1983.00)	320.00 (8889.00)

Note: Figures in parentheses indicate percentages with first plan figures as base.
Source: For First Plan to Sixth Plan Report of KVIC/1985-86 Bombay, 1986.

EIGHTH FIVE YEAR PLAN

In the Eighth Five Year Plan, the Government decision is to allocate 50 per cent of the plan investment to the Rural and Agricultural development, shrinking of the plan size will mean even less of investment for the infrastructure especially power which is key input both for the agricultural and industrial development (i.e.) cottage and small scale industries.

A major change proposed in the Eighth Plan is to redefine the Rural and Agricultural sector. There is a growing realisation that if these heads of expenditure are taken out of the purview of Rural and Agricultural development, which includes cottage and small scale industries those are highly labour intensive through self employment the total allocation to these sectors will amount to more than 60 per cent of the total public sector investment.

INDUSTRIAL DEVELOPMENT IN BACKWARD REGIONS IN INDIA POLICIES AND PROGRAMMES FOR THE DEVELOPMENT OF SMALL SCALE INDUSTRIES IN INDIA

The Small Industries have enough scope to exploit available local resources such as savings, raw materials, skilled and un-skilled labour. Further, they generate income for consumption of wage goods and provide employment to the unemployed persons. So, it is necessary to allot public sector investment for development of infrastructural facilities and provide incentives through developmental programmes for setting up of small industries.

The Industries Policy Resolution, 1948 stressed the need for development of Small Scale Industries. The objectives of the policy are:

1. To establish a social order where justice and equality of opportunities could be assured
2. To raise the standard of living of the people through exploitation of talents and available resources of the country.
3. To accelerate production to meet the needs of the growing population and
4. To provide more and more opportunities for employment. This policy was in force upto 1956.

During the First Five Year Plan, a major step was taken for the development of village and small industries. It was the establishment of six All India Boards to advise and assist the Government in the formulation of programmes for development of handloom industry, Khadi and Village industries, small scale industries, Handicrafts, Sericulture an International Team of experts was invited by the Government of India in 1953 to study the problems of the small scale industries. The team recommended the establishment of Regional Small Industries Service Institutes. Accordingly four such Institutes were set up at Bombay, Calcutta, Madurai and Faridabad with branch units in Uttar Pradesh, Bihar, Andhra Pradesh and

Travancore Cochin. These Institutes provide various kinds of technical services to village and small industries, such as, information about improved techniques of production, technical advice and assistance in the utilisation of the local raw materials.[17] The programme of work of the Small Scale Industries Board follows largely the lines indicated in the Report of the International Team. The main part of the programme was the establishment of a number of Institutes for organisation, technical servicing and business counselling and marketing assistance.

Industrial Estates

The Industrial Estates Programme was started in 1955 following the recommendation of the International Planning Team. Under this programme, suitable sites with all the facilities, such as, water, electricity, transport, steam, communications, banks, post-office, Aid etc., are to be provided so as to create the necessary climate for the development of small industries. The main objectives of the Industrial Estate Programme are:

1. To shift the small scale industries from congested areas to Industrial Estates with a view to increasing their productivity.
2. To achieve decentralised industrial development in small towns and villages and
3. To assist ancillary industries in the townships surrounding major industrial undertakings, both in the public and private sectors.[18]

The Government of India had given a big boost under different Five Year Plans by encouraging the establishment of Industrial Estates in the country. The expenditure incurred during the plan periods by the Central and State Government on Industrial Estates is presented below:

Table 2.3

Expenditure Incurred on Industrial Estates in India (Rs. in crores)

S.No.	Plan	Period	S.S.I.	Industrial	Total
1.	First	1951-56	5.20	0.58	5.78
2.	Second	1956-61	44.40	11.60	56.00
3.	Third	1961-66	90.91	22.15	113.06
4.	Annual	1966-69	45.90	7.58	53.48
5.	Fourth	1969-74	80.46	15.73	96.19
6.	Fifth	1974-79	196.12	25.62	221.74
7.	Annual	1979-80	95.69	9.12	104.81
8.	Sixth	1980-85	561.74	54.36	616.10
9.	Seventh	1985-90	–	–	1120.51

Source: Government of India, Development Commissioner Small Scale Industry, New Delhi, Ministry of Industry.

From the above Table 2.3 it can be observed that the expenditure incurred for the development of industrial estates has increased significantly from a mere Rs. 0.58 crores in the First Plan to Rs. 54.36 crores in the Sixth Plan. It indicates that the amount spent for industrial infrastructure has increased impressively.

Industrial Development of Backward Areas

A serious thought was given by our policy makers, after Independence to make all the regions industrially developed so that greater employment opportunities and economic avocations can be provided to the people. The Government, since 1968, has been specially trying to stimulate the industrialisation of the backward areas. As a sequence to this policy decision, the Central Government appointed two Committees popularly known as "Pande Committee"[19] and "Wanchoo Committee"[20] Pande Committee was asked to go into the aspect of identifying industrially backward states and backward districts in the States, while the Wanchoo Committee was asked to suggest the financial and physical incentives to be given for promotion of new industries in industrially backward states. The Planning Commission approved the recommendations made by these Committees, with certain modifications as per the decisions taken by the

National Development Council. Finally, the Planning Commission in consultation with the financial institutions recommended to the State Government for implementation of the schemes of concessional finance and fiscal incentives. As a result, 246 districts all over the country were now eligible for concessional finance under the scheme. Out of these, 102 districts or areas have been selected for Central Investment Subsidy. Under the scheme of Backward Area Development, certain facilities, such as capital investment, subsidy, transport subsidy, credit, machinery on hire-purchase and also state incentives were provided by the Government directly or through some agencies for promotion of small scale industries in backward areas.

The Central Government Capital Investment Subsidy Scheme was introduced in 1971, after considering the recommendations of Wanchoo Committee by the 'National Development Council'. Under this scheme, new or expanding units in selected backward districts were entitled to 10% subsidy on the total fixed capital or additional fixed capital investment upto Rs. 50 lakhs. However units with investment exceeding this ceiling would also be considered at the discretion of the Government, though the maximum amount of subsidy would still be Rs. 5 lakhs. In 1973, the rate of subsidy was raised to 15% the investment Ceiling to Rs. 1 crore. The discretionary clause for Units with investment exceeding this limit would still hold, subject to a subsidy limit of Rs. 15 lakhs.

Simultaneously with the capital investment subsidy, a transport subsidy scheme was also introduced in 1971 to develop industries in hilly backward areas. Under this scheme, new industrial units in the states and Union Territories of Jammu and Kashmir, Assam, Manipur, Meghalaya, Nagaland, Tripura, Arunachal Pradesh, Mizoram, Andaman and Nicobar Islands, Lakshadeep, Himachal Pradesh and the hilly districts of Uttar Pradesh were eligible to a subsidy amounting to 50% of the transportation costs of both raw materials and finished goods. Expanding units were also eligible for this subsidy for their expansion programmes, provided that the increase in production exceeded 25% of average annual output during the last three years.

Credit facilities do have a vital role in the implementation of small industries development programmes. The availability of required credit on easy and liberal terms is also essential for the progress of small industries. To achieve this, sound institutional frame work is essential for the flow of credit to the small industries. The existing institutional framework for the flow of financial assistance to the small scale industries sector consists of Banks (Commercial Banks, Co-operative Banks and Regional Rural Banks). State Financial Corporations (SFC's), National Small Industrial Corporation (NSIC) and State Small Scale Industries Development Corporations (SSIDC). The Industrial Development Bank of India (IDBI) provides funds to the Comercial Banks and State Financial Corporations (SFC's) through refinancing and bills rediscounting schemes.

The Industrial Development Bank of India set up a Small and Village Industries wing in 1978 to evolve appropriate policy framework to identify action areas for promoting the growth of the small and village industries and to monitor the credit facilities offered by various agencies of this sector. The refinance facility of Industrial Development Bank of India (IDBI) was and is even now channelled through 180 primary lending institutions, which comprise 70 scheduled Commercial Banks, 56 Regional Rural Banks, 10 State Co-operative Banks, 18 State Finance Corporation, 24 SIDC's and two All India Financial Institutions.[22]

INDUSTRIALISATION

Industrialisation has been defined by Sutcliffe as a process which has invariably been the "outcome or accompaniment of economic development, a set of policies, which more than any other set of policies is seen as a means towards economic development."[25] Industrialisation in a developing country has become inseparable part of development process. Planners and policy makers have viewed it as the most acceptable instrument to generate dynamism in growth process. It has been argued that in an underdeveloped country with a backward agriculture and vast population there is a little choice but to give priority to the development of industries. The establishment of new kind of society (Industrialised) is easier than reformation of old"[24].

It is so because, the Industrial Sector is more powerful in innovation which injects dynamism and brings about lasting increase in productivity of labour. "Industrialisation not only influences the growth of national output and income but also influences the natural life and the social, political and cultural pattern". Industrialisation of a basically agricultural primary export oriented economy as seen as the means by which the chains of dependance forced during the colonical period could be broken matching the newly acquired political independence with economic independence.[25] For these newly freed underdeveloped countries, industrialisation was sought to bring great relief. "It was hoped that Industrialisation would bring social transformation, social equality, higher levels of employment, more equitable distribution of income and well balanced regional development."[26] Industrial development has further been acknowledged as a means to distribute employment, income and consumption between the various regions by giving special emphasis on industrialisation of backward regions. In the opinion of Rosestein Rodan Industrialisation is the way of achieving a more equal distribution of income between different areas of the world by raising income in depressed areas at a higher rate than in rich areas.[27] What Rosenstein Rodan says in the context of world economy is also applicable to an individual country, suffering from the problems of inter regional as well as intra regional disparities in development. Development of Industries in backward regions, therefore has been accepted as a means to reduce regional disparities. It is because, in addition to its innovation and dynamism that it is more flexible than agriculture as far as location aspect is considered. Manufacturing activity which is not rooted to raw material can be located in any region even in areas with poor natural endowment if it is economically feasible to serve objective. Moreover, manufacturing activities have better potentiality for generating employment directly and indirectly through their backward and forward linkages with other sectors of the economy, most effective in raising productively of labour which is very essential for economic development. Use of local raw material, employment of local labour, skilled and unskilled, would create an impact on income levels and pull the region out of its backwardness and promote regionally balanced development.

Policy to promote industries in Backward Regions in India

Though India embarked on developmental planning in 1950 the concern for the disparities in regional development was found, for the first time, in its Industrial Policy Resolution in 1956. Which stressed the necessity to reduce disparities in industrial development through faster industrialisation of backward areas. However, little was done during the First and Second Plans. It was the Third Five Year Plan, which strongly drew the attention to the problem of regional disparities. The Third Five Year Plan document contained a special chapter on balanced regional development. It was stated in the Third Plan Summary Document that the development of regions and of the national economy as a whole have to be viewed as part of the same process. The progress of the national economy will be reflected in the rate of growth realised by different regions and in turn greater development of the resources in the regions must contribute towards acclerating the rate of progress in the country as whole.[28] In order to achieve this goal, the third plan suggested the measures which included extensive development of agriculture, extension of irrigation, the programme of village and small industries, the large scale expansion of power development of road and road transport etc.

But the steps taken by the Government during the Third Plan Period could not reduce the regional disparities. In fact these disparities became wider which caused anxiety to the Government. The Fourth Five Year Plan (1969-74) admitted. "The social and economic costs of servicing large concentration of population are prohibitive, beyond a certain limit unit costs of providing utilities and services increased rapidly with increase in the size of the cities. In the ultimate analysis problem is that of planning the spatial location of economic activity throughout the country. A beginning must be made by tackling the problems of larger cities and taking positive steps for dispersal through suitable creation of small centres in the rest of the areas.[29]

This concern of the Government about the regional disparities and inequality in income and employment initiated it to take same measures to remove. How to set right the regional imbalances and the planning for development of backward region did start during the Fourth Five Year Plan. During the Fourth Five Year Plan certain changes in distribution of central assistance was introduced which was based on the criteria like population, tax effort, per capita state income requirements of irritation and power projects etc. District and area plans were also considered essential for ensuring optimal distribution and utilisation of resources to reduce disparities between different areas and segments of population.

In the Fifth Five Year Plan (1974-79) emphasis was put on the development of backward areas through special programme like hill area development programmes Integrated Tribal Areas Development Programme etc., with view to redistribute personal income.

In the Six Five Year Plan (1980-85) reduction of regional disparities became a parallel objective of Indian Planning, through progressive reduction inequalities and diffusion in technological benefits. Sixth Plan, therefore, stated that "the measures to be pursued for reduction of regional inequalities have to be consistent with the general objective of achieving a SPC growth in the economy as a whole".[30] There was a change in the emphasis on the role of states in implementing the policy in the direction of reducing regional disparities. The Plan emphatically states that backwardness does not recognise state boundaries and it may be necessary over time to take account of this in the policies concerning resource transfer relatively richer states need to pay adequate attention to the backward areas with in their territories and the claims of the backward states must also be sustained for the basis of proven programmes for the benefit of backward regions.[31] This statement clearly indicates the increasing role of the State in the coming years in respect of development of backward regions Government policy during 6th Plan. It was highly influenced by the recommendation of the National Committee on the backward areas development (Under the Chairmanship of B. Shivaraman) which submitted its report to the Government in 1981.

Criteria for the Identification of Backward Area

Though successive Five Year Plans placed emphasis on balanced development, it was only in 1968 that concrete action was taken by the Central Government. The National Development Council (NDC) in its meeting held on 12th September, 1968 decided that two working groups should be set up for studying the question of regional imbalances. In pursuance of this decision, two working groups were set up by the planning commission; One for recommending the criteria for the identification of backward areas under the Chairmanship of B.D. Pande and the other for recommending the fiscal and financial incentives for starting industries in the backward areas under the chairmanship of N.N. Wanchoo.

The Pande working Group recommended that the following criteria to be applied in aggregate for the purpose of identification of industrially backward states and Union Territories. (a) Total Per Capital Income, (b) Per Capita Income from industry and mining, (c) Number of workers in registered factories (d) Per capita annual consumption of electricity (e) length of surfaced roads in relation to population and the area of the states and (f) railway mileage in relation to population and the area of the State.

On the basis of these criteria, the provide group recommended and the Government of India approved that the following industrially backward states and Union Territories should qualify for special treatment by way of incentives for industrial development.

Incentives for Development of Backward Area

The Wanchoo Working Group recommended the following set of fiscal incentives for attracting the entrepreneurs to set up industries in the backward area:[33]

a) Grant of higher development rebate to industries located in backward areas.
b) Grant of exemption from Income-tax, including corporate tax for 5 years after providing for the development rebate
c) Exemption from import duties on plant and machinery component, etc., imported by units set up in backward areas
d) Exemption from excise duties for a period of five years
e) Exemption from sales tax, both on raw materials and finished products to units set up in specified backward areas for a period of five years from the date of their going into production and
f) Transport subsidy.

We feel that there is a case for giving transport subsidy to reasons for special remoteness of certain areas, for taking out the finished products for a period of 5 years up to 400 miles, the distance should be considered as normal and beyond that the transportation cost for finished products should be subsidised for such backward areas as maybe selected in the States of Assam, Nagaland, Manipur, Tripura, NEFA and Andamans. The Transport subsidy should be equivalent to 50 per cent of the cost of transportation in case of the backward areas specified in Jammu and Kahmir State.[34]

The Criteria for the selection of the industrially backward districts in the State and Union Territories were to be decided by the Planning Commission in consultation with the Financial Institutions and the State Government, in the light of the two sets of criteria recommended by the Panda Committee. The following set of criteria was involved by the Planning Commission for the purpose of identification of industrially backward districts to quality for concessional finance:[35]

a) Per capita food grains or commercial crops production depending as whether the district is predominantly a producer of food grains of cash crops
b) Ratio of agricultural workers to population
c) Per capita industrial output (gross)
d) Number of factory employees per lakh of population or alternatively number of persons engaged in the secondary and territory activities per lakh of population
e) Length of surfaced roads in relation to population or railway mileage in relation to population.

Identification of Backward Areas

Six Point Formula

With a view to maintaining the integrity of the State against the background of certain political unrest in the State, the Government of India announced a six point formula in 1973. In accordance with the formula the Government of India agreed to make available a special assistance of Rs. 90 crores for the accelerated development of the backward areas in the State during Fifth Plan which, necessitated the identification of backward areas.

After the special central assistance came to an end by the end of Fifth Plan, the Government of Andhra Pradesh constituted a technical committee to advise the Government on the Criteria to be adopted for the identification of the backward areas in the States and other technical issues related to the problems such as unit of identification etc.

Identification of Backward Taluqs

In conformity with the objective of the National Planning the removal or atleast reduction of regional imbalances in development is an important objective of the Sixth Five Year Plan of Andhra Pradesh. In this context accelerated development of backward areas and target groups assume importance[37] while at the national level, the State could be considered as a unit for assessing the relative levels of development and evolving policies for reducing the disparities between these units, at the State level also there is need to study the existence of disparities with in the State among its regions. Despite the development achieved in various sectors during the past Five Year Plan periods, regional disparities still persist both at National and State levels. In the context of removal of regional imbalances, the identification of backward areas assumes considerable importance, since it is only by a policy of accelerated development of such areas that regional imbalances can be removed or atleast reduced. In the context, the Planning Department of the Government of Andhra Pradesh had undertaken a number of exercises in the past for identifying the backward areas. The first of such exercise in the state was with reference to the identification of drought affected taluqs. The committee identified 118 taluqs for being eligible to be classified as backward, the region-wise break up are coastal Andhra 35, Rayalseema 24 and Telangana.[39]

The Committee, therefore, recommended to the State Government to accept and declare 118 taluqs, shown in Appendix as backward for allocating any special funds/assistance for the development of such areas.

GROWTH OF SMALL SCALE INDUSTRIES IN ANDHRA PRADESH

The District Industries Centre have been setup in the State of Andhra Pradesh in 3 phases—the first phase with effect from 1-12-1978 covering 11 districts, the second phase from 1-7-1979 covering 3 districts and the third phase from 1-3-1981 covering the rest of the 8 districts. However, the District Industries Centres started for implementing the programmes from April, 1980. Each District Industries Centre was originally conceived to have a staffing pattern of one general manager in the cadre of joint director, supported by 7 functional managers in the cardre of Deputy Director in the disciplines as instructed by the Government of India. Subsequently it has been modified to have 4 functional managers in the disciplines as communicated by the Government of India. According to the restructured used staffing pattern, the State Government have created one post of general manager, supported by 4 functional managers to look after the disciplines economic investigation and infrastructure, credit village industries and training and raw material and marketing. The State Government also sanctioned 10 posts of project managers at each District Industries Centre in the districts of Srikakulam, East Godavari, Krishna, Prakasam, Chittoor, Anantapur, Karimnagar, Nalgonda, Medak and Ranga Reddy. The Project Managers act as technical specialists in the District Industries Centres relevant to the needs of the districts. At the block level, extension officers are working to identify the artisan candidates and entrepreneurs during the credit campaigns and arrange training programmes, electrification in the traders like auto-mechanism, tailoring, mat weaving, matches manufacturing, leather, tanning, typewriting, radio and T.V. mechanism through various promotional institutions under different schemes. Stipends are provided to the candidates during training. Entrepreneurs are also selected for improvement of skills, talents and managerial abilities through training programmes conducted by the Andhra Pradesh Productivity Council, Small Industries Service Institute, Small Industries Extension Training Institute (APITCO), Andhra Pradesh Small Scale Industrial Development Corporation (APSSIDC) and State Finance Corporation (SFC).

DISTRICT-WISE UNITS, FIXED CAPITAL AND EMPLOYMENT BEFORE AND AFTER INCEPTION OF DISTRICT INDUSTRIES CENTRES

The district-wise analysis of small scale industrial units, fixed capital and employment is undertaken to study the variations in the growth of these variables after the inception of DIC. The table 2.4 shows the details relating to these aspects.

Before inception of District Industries Centres there were 30342 small scale units functioning in the state. By 1988 the number of units have risen to 65832, showing an increase of 47 per cent. Fixed capital has

Table 2.4
Product-wise Growth of Units, Fixed Capital and Employment

Sl. No.	Industry group	Before Inception of DIC (upto 1979)			After Inception of DIC March, 1988			Percentage Change		
		Units	Fixed Capital (Rs. in Crores)	Employment	Units	Fixed Capital (Rs. in Crores)	Employment	Units	Fixed Capital (Rs. in Crores)	Employment
1	2	3	4	5	6	7	8	9	10	11
1.	Food Products	7363	46.27	87755	16773	150.12	153594	228	324	175
2.	Beverages and Tabacco Products	371	3.20	24408	807	7.38	31493	218	231	129
3.	Cotton Textiles	535	6.17	18735	949	15.14	32346	117	245	173
4.	Wool, Silk and Synth Fibre Textile	42	0.26	499	59	0.54	650	140	208	130
5.	June, Hemp and Mesta Products	13	0.10	557	30	0.17	660	231	170	118
6.	Hosiery and Garments	639	1.48	8991	1346	5.70	14522	211	385	162
7.	Wood Products	2514	3.04	16124	5112	10.42	29840	203	264	185
8.	Paper Products and Printing	2347	11.67	17007	4498	31.65	28242	192	271	166
9.	Leather Products	691	1.50	4274	1611	3.65	8733	233	243	204
10.	Rubber and Plastic Products	1027	6.52	9237	2994	31.84	20872	292	488	226

1	2	3	4	5	6	7	8	9	10	11
11.	Chemical and Chemical Products	1729	13.96	22754	3143	47.15	37641	182	338	165
12.	Non Metalic Mineral Products	2418	9.28	35716	5348	42.48	79565	221	458	223
13.	Basic Metal Industries	495	8.13	9759	1022	27.58	17565	206	339	180
14.	Metal Products	4368	12.79	32377	7724	28.56	52508	177	223	162
15.	Machinery and Parts except Electrical	2085	11.10	15457	4864	30.45	29876	233	274	193
16.	Electrical Machinery	509	4.39	6753	1451	15.44	14169	285	352	210
17.	Transport Equipment and Parts	438	1.80	3715	801	4.30	6890	183	239	185
18.	Misc. Manufacturing Industries	477	2.05	4292	940	6.78	6891	197	282	161
19.	Repairs and Servicing	2281	6.01	12028	6360	21.09	27756	279	351	231
	Total	30342	150.62	330438	65832	479.45	593817	217	318	180

Source: Government of Andhra Pradesh, Hyderabad, Commissioner of Industries.

increased more rapidly from Rs. 150.62 crores to over Rs. 479.44 crores by 218 per cent. Thus, the starting of DICs has produced a posetime effect not only on the number of units functioning but also on fixed capital and employment.

District-wise analysis suggests that both before and after the inception of District Industries Centres, there were inter district variations in respect of number of units, fixed capital and employment. Before the inception of District Industries Centres in 8 districts Vijayawada, East Godavari, West Godavari, Krishna, Guntur, Prakasam, Nellore, Anantapur and Hyderabad, the number of units functioning was above the state average. On the otherhand in the districts of Srikakulam, Vijayanagaram, Mahaboobnagar, Rangareddy, Medak, Nizamabad, Adilabad, Warangal and Nalgonda, the number of units functioning was far below the State average, Similar trend was observed in respect of fixed capital and employment. In seven districts the average fixed capital and average employment were above the state average.

After inception of District Industries Centres, the number of districts above the state average has gone upto nine in the case of units functioning and employment, while in respect of fixed capital the number remained at seven. After the establishment of District Industries Centres, a considerable progress has been achieved in all these respects in all the regions of the state. However, the progress in different regions has been uneven. In coastal Andhra regions through the progress has been uneven the number of units has risen by 116 per cent, while fixed capital and employment have increased by 188 per cent and 78 per cent respectively. The corresponding percentage increases in the number of units fixed capital and employment were 89, 181 and 65 respectively for Rayalaseema and 130, 252 and 80 respectively for Telangana. A study of district-wise shares in total number of units fixed capital and employment in the state before and after the setting up of District Industries Centres will throw light on changes in their shares and policy of the Government towards backward regions. The

Table 2.5

Disctirct-wise Percentage of Variation of Small Scale Industrial Units, Fixed Capital and Employment

Sl. No.	Industry group	Before Inception of DIC (upto 1979)			After Inception of DIC March, 1988			Percentage Change of variation after Inception of DICs		
		Units	Fixed Capital	Employment	Units	Fixed Capital	Employment	Units	Fixed Capital	Employment
1	2	3	4	5	6	7	8	9	10	11
I.	**Coastal Region**									
1.	Srikakulam	1.90	1.19	1.77	3.28	1.93	2.65	+1.38	+0.74	+0.88
2.	Vizianagaran	1.40	1.22	1.57	2.77	1.57	2.25	+1.37	+0.35	+0.68
3.	Visakhapatnam	3.44	3.21	3.41	5.12	3.54	4.49	+1.68	+0.13	+1.08
4.	East Godavari	6.45	5.45	6.03	5.98	5.00	5.96	-0.47	-0.45	-0.07
5.	West Godavari	5.40	4.54	6.03	4.97	4.43	5.30	-0.43	-0.01	-0.73
6.	Krishna	9.49	8.56	7.40	7.54	6.72	6.64	-1.85	-1.84	-0.76
7.	Guntur	6.42	6.72	9.43	5.53	4.92	8.28	0.89	-1.80	-1.15
8.	Prakasam	4.62	2.60	4.82	4.66	2.02	5.18	+0.04	+0.22	+0.36
9.	Nellore	5.65	4.05	2.23	4.58	2.98	3.56	-1.07	-1.07	-0.67
Total		44.77	37.54	44.67	44.53	33.91	44.31	-0.24	-3.62	-0.36

{Cont.}.....

1	2	3	4	5	6	7	8	9	10	11
II. Rayalseema Region										
10.	Chittor	4.16	2.72	2.90	3.36	3.57	2.88	-0.80	+0.85	-0.02
11.	Cuddapah	3.87	3.79	3.49	3.83	2.53	3.08	-0.04	-1.26	-0.41
12.	Anatapur	4.43	3.40	3.61	3.49	2.66	3.06	-0.94	-0.74	-0.55
13.	Kurnool	3.44	3.32	3.65	3.16	2.91	3.50	-0.28	-0.42	-0.15
	Total	15.90	13.23	13.67	13.84	11.67	12.52	-0.26	-1.57	-1.15
III. Telengana Region										
14.	Mahaboob Nagar	2.35	1.86	1.34	2.92	3.55	1.93	+0.67	+1.69	+0.59
15.	Ranga Reddy	2.92	7.56	4.21	5.73	14.05	7.57	+2.81	+6.49	+3.36
16.	Hyderabad	16.04	22.04	16.57	11.09	10.62	12.11	-4.95	-11.42	-4.46
17.	Medak	3.02	4.99	3.93	3.53	9.43	4.78	+1.51	+4.44	+0.85
18.	Nizamabad	2.29	2.38	4.43	2.88	2.24	3.98	+0.59	-0.14	-0.45
19.	Adilabad	1.59	2.14	2.84	1.54	1.57	2.12	-0.05	0.57	0.72
20.	Kariamnagar	1.34	1.91	2.18	3.72	3.21	2.63	0.38	+1.30	+0.45

{Cont.}...

1 2	3	4	5	6	7	8	9	10	11
21. Warangal	2.60	1.83	2.03	3.02	2.97	2.62	0.42	+1.14	+0.59
22. Khammam	3.35	2.20	1.84	3.75	2.58	2.43	0.40	+0.38	+0.59
23. Nalgonda	2.93	2.32	2.29	3.45	4.20	3.00	0.52	+1.88	+0.61
Total	39.33	49.23	41.66	41.63	54.42	43.17	2.30	+5.19	+1.51
Andhra Pradesh	100.00	100.00	100.00	100.00	100.00	100.00	-	-	-

Source: Government of Andhra Pradesh, Hyderabad, Commissioner of Industries.

developed districts are those whose percentage share was above 4.35 in respect of number of units, fixed capital and employment and district whose percentage share is below these are considered to be less developed districts, the table 2.5 shows the details.

The table 2.5 shows that after setting up of District Industries Centres there has been an increase in the percentage share with regard to number of units, fixed capital and employment in all the less developed districts with the exception of Anantapur, Chittoor, Cuddapah and Kurnool in Rayalseema region, Nellore in coastal Andhra region and Adilabad in Telangana region. In the developed districts the percentage share in respect of units, fixed capital and employment has declined after inception of DICs, exception being the districts of Ranga Reddy and Medak districts where the shares have substantially improved. This may perhaps be due to the proximity of the districts to Hyderabad where all facilities provided by the promotional institutions are available.

PRODUCT-WISE GROWTH OF UNITS, FIXED CAPITAL AND EMPLOYMENT AFTER INCEPTION OF DISTRICT INDUSTRIES CENTRES

Product-wise analysis of the growth of units, fixed capital and employment will be useful in the study of the effects of District Industries Centres in different categories of industries. The details relating to these aspects are shown in the table 2.6.

The table 2.6 shows that there was more than a one fold increase in most of the categories of industries after inception of District Industries Centres, in number of units and fixed capital and about two fold increase in the case of employment the growth was substantially higher in rubber and plastic products, non metallic mineral products, wool-silk and synthetic fibre textiles and jute, hemp and mesta products. It shows that within a period of a tittle over 8 years after the District Industries Centres have been setup there was a rapid growth in terms of units, fixed capital and employment.

Table 2.6
Disctirct-wise Units, Fixed Capital and Employment

Sl. No.	Industry group	Before Inception of DIC			After Inception of DIC			Percentage Change		
		Units	Fixed Capital Rs. 000'	Employment	Units	Fixed Capital Rs. 000'	Employment	Units	Invest-ment	Employment
1	2	3	4	5	6	7	8	9	10	11
I.	Coastal Region									
1.	Srikakulam	575	17895	5845	2157	92798	15759	275	415	170
2.	Vizianagaram	426	18417	5170	1823	74922	13310	328	307	157
3.	Visakhapatnam	1044	48291	11264	3373	170015	26667	223	252	137
4.	East Godavari	1958	82079	19920	3934	239769	35380	101	192	78
5.	West Godavari	1640	68363	19919	3271	212311	31454	100	211	58
6.	Krishna	2881	128953	24461	5034	322393	39439	75	150	61
7.	Guntur	1947	101272	31159	3641	235848	49171	87	133	58
8.	Prakasam	1403	39121	15922	3070	135337	30782	119	246	93
9.	Nellore	1713	61056	13986	3014	142659	21161	76	134	51
	Total	13587	165447	147646	29317	1626052	263123	116	188	78

{Cont.}.....

1	2	3	4	5	6	7	8	9	10	11
II. Rayalseema Region										
10.	Chittor	1262	40925	9582	2210	171139	17034	75	318	78
11.	Cuddapah	1173	57051	11542	2521	121205	18036	115	113	59
12.	Anatapur	1344	51241	11976	2298	127502	18191	71	149	52
13.	Kurnool	1044	50008	12062	2080	139237	20789	99	178	72
Total		4823	199223	45162	9109	559083	74320	89	181	65
III. Telengana Region										
14.	Mahaboob Nagar	683	28052	4437	1920	170285	11461	81	507	158
15.	Ranga Reddy	885	113819	13910	3776	673525	44962	327	492	223
16.	Hyderabad	4866	331968	54753	7301	509573	71932	50	54	31
17.	Medak	613	75219	12994	2322	452174	28414	279	501	119
18.	Nizamabad	695	35885	14654	1895	106977	23644	173	198	61
19.	Adilabad	481	32190	9392	1016	74100	12599	111	133	34
20.	Karimnagar	1014	28775	7199	2449	154108	15608	142	436	117
21.	Warangal	788	27557	6696	1991	142427	15487	152	417	131

{Cont.}...

1	2	3	4	5	6	7	8	9	10	11
22.	Khammam	1017	33187	6075	2468	123502	14446	143	172	138
23.	Nalgonda	890	34900	7580	2268	201546	17281	155	477	135
	Total	11932	741552	137690	27406	2609217	256374	130	252	86
	Andhra Pradesh	30342	1506224	330498	65832	4794352	593817	117	218	80
	X	1319	65488	14370	2862	208450	25818			

Source: Government of Andhra Pradesh, Hyderabad, Commissioner of Industries.

CONCLUSION

The performance of District Industries Centres in the State of Andhra Pradesh is relatively better when compared to that of District Industries Centres in the country as a whole. However, inter and intra-district variations continue to exist even after the setting up of District Industries Centers in the state, even though the concentration of units, fixed capital and employment has declined to some extent in recent times. Further, the small scale industries units in the state are confronting certain problems, same with the preview of District Industries Centres and others beyond their control. Unless the lapses within and outside District Industries Centres are eliminated the very objective of establishing District Industries Centres in state will be defeated.

UNION TERRITORIES

All Union Territories except Chandigarh, Delhi and Pondicherry.

Subsequently, Meghalaya, Himachal Pradesh and Sikkim and the Union Territory of Pondicherry were added to the above list. The Pande Group also recommended the following criteria or indicators of backwardness, for identification of backward districts in backward states, Union Territories:

(a) District should be outside a radius of about 50 miles from larger cities and large industrial projects
(b) Poverty of the people as indicated by low per capita income starting from the lowest to 25% below the state average
(c) High density of population in relation to utilisation of productive resources and employment opportunities as indicated by
   (i) Low percentage of population engaged in secondary and tertiary activities (25% below the state average may be considered as backward

(ii) Low percentage of factory employment (25% below the state average may be considered as backward

(iii) Non or under utilisation of economic and natural resources like minerals, forests etc.

(iv) Adequate availability of electric power or likelihood of its availability within the next one or two years

(v) Availability transport and communication facilities or likelihood of their availability within the next one or two years, and

(vi) Adequate availability of water or likelihood of its availability with in the one or two years. The Pande Group felt that about 20 to 30 districts in all may be finally selected for grant of special incentives during the Fourth Plan Period. The group had suggested that such districts should have a potential for development so that efforts could be concentrated on these selected districts in the first instance, and gradually extended to all the remaining districts.

Table 2.7
Industry Backward Districts, State-wise Summary

State/Union Territories		Backward district	
		Percentage of total area of the state	Total population of the state
Developed (A)			
West Bengal	13	82	68
Tamil Nadu	8	64	60
Gujarat	10	67	49
Maharashtra	13	54	42
Punjab	4	39	35
Harayana	4	30	39
Karnataka	11	67	63
Kerala	5	42	52
Total (A)			
Backward (B)			
Andhra Pradesh	14	72	59
Bihar	9	47	55
Rajasthan	16	62	54
Madhya Pradesh	36	87	83
Assam	7	78	76
Uttar Pradesh	37	68	62
Orissa	8	61	48
Jammu & Kashmir	10	100	100
Nagaland	3	100	100
Himachal Pradesh	7	88	73
Manipur	5	100	100
Meghalaya	2	100	100
Tripura	3	100	100
Goa, Daman & Diu	3	100	
Pondicherry	4	100	
Andaman & Nicobar Islands	1	100	
Arunachal Pradesh	5	100	
Dadar & Nagar Haveli	1	100	
Lakshadeep	1	69	
Mizoram			
Total (B)		71	58

All India * the number of districts declined has seen risen to 247.
Source: Ministry of Industrial Development, Guidelines for industry 1984-85, June, 84.

APPENDIX

1. (a) Accelerated development of the backward areas of the State. Planned Development of State Capital with special resources earmarked for these purposes.
   (b) Association of representatives of such backward areas other experts in the formulation of development schemes.
   (c) Constitution of a State Level Planning Board and sub committees for different backward areas.
2. (a) Preference to local candidates in the matter of admissions to educational institutions.
   (b) Establishment of a new Central University at Hyderabad to augment the existing educational facilities.
3. Local candidates given preference in the matter of direct recruitment to
   a) Non-Gazetted Posts (Other than those in the secretariat under Heads of Departments and in the State level officers Hyderabad City Police).
   b) Corresponding posts under the local bodies.
   c) The posts of Tahsildars, Junior Engineers and Civil Assistants Surgeons.
4. Constitution of a high power Administrative Tribunal to deal with the grievances of the services in matters of appointment seniority, promotion etc. This would limit resource to the judiciary.
5. Necessary Constitutional amendments be enchanced to avoid litigations and uncertainity.
6. Abolition of Multi Rules and Regional Committees.

A. Coastal Region

1. Vishkhapatnam Districts

Anakapalli, Yellamanchli, Gajapathinagaram, Narsipatnam, Chodavaram, Samarlakota, Bheemunipatnam, Vizianagaram, Chintapalli, Paderu, Vishkahapatnam.

2. East Godavari District

Yellavaram, Peddapuram, Prathipadu, Tuni, Pithapuram.

3. West Godavari District

Polavaram, Chintalapudi.

4. Krishna District

Nandigama, Jaggayapeta, Tiruvuru, Backward Taluqs, Nuzivedu.

5. Guntur District

Vinukonda, Palnadu, Sattenappli.

6. Nellore District

Gudur, Sullurpet, Venkatagiri, Rapur, Atmakur, Udayagiri, Kavali.

7. Prakasam District

Ongole, Kandukuru, Kanigiri, Padili, Darsi, Addanki, Markapur, Giddalur.

B. Rayalaseema Region

1. Chittoor District

Palamaneru, Kuppam, Punganur, Madanapalli, Vayalpad, Satyavedu, Chittoor, Banaganipalli, Srikalashsti, Puttur, (Pulivendula, Kamalapuram).

2. Cuddapah District

Rayachoti, Jammalamadugu, Badwel.

3. Anantapur District

Kalyandurg, Uravakonda, Rayadurg, Dharmavaram, Kadiri, Penukonda, Hindupur, Madakasira.

4. Kurnool District

Nandikotkur, Atmakur, Allagadda, Koilkuntla, Pattikonda, Alur, Adoni, Kurnool.

C. Telangana Region

1.Mahaboob Nagar District

Achampet, Kollapur Nagar, Kurnool, Wanaparthi, Alampur, Gadwal, Makthal, Atmakur, Kadangal.

2.Hyderabad District

Ibrahimpatnam, Chevelli, Parti, Tandur, Vikarabad, Medchal.

3.Medak District

Sanga Reddy, Narayana, Adndole, Gadwal, Siddipet.

4. Nizamabad District

Yellareddi, Madnoor, Banswada.

5. Adilabad District

Adilabad, Asifabad, Sirpur, Chennur, Luneetipet, Khananapur, Boath, Mudhole, Nirmal.

6. Karimnagar District

Metpalle, Jagtial, Peddapalle, Karimnagar, Sicilla, Manthani, Huzurabad.

7. Warangal District

Warangal, Parkal, Mulugu, Narasampet, Mahaboobad, Jangoon.

8. Khammam District

Madhera

9. Nalgonda District

Ramannapet, Bhongir, Devarakonda, Suryapet

LIST OF 118 TALUQS IDENTIFIED AS BACKWARD

a) Coastal Region

Srikakulam

Narasannapeta, Salur, Bobbili, Palthapatnam, Parvathipuram, Palkonda, Chepurpally.

Visakhapatnam

Ellamanchali, Bheemunipatnam, Chodavaram, S.Kota, Narsipatnam, Gajapathinagaram, Chintapally Panderu.

East Godavari

Chitalapudi, Polavaram

Krishna

Tiruruvu, Nandigamma, Kaikalur.

Guntur

Sattenapalle, Palnad, Vinukonda.

Kurnool

Dhone, Nandikottur, Allgadda, Koilakuntla, Pattikonda, Alur.

Medak

Medak, Zaheerabad, Gajwal, Narasapur, Andole, Narayanaked, Siddipet.

Mahaboob Nagar

Shadnagar, Gawal, Nagarkurnool, Kedangal, Kalvakurthy, Achampet, Alampur, Killapur, 'Wargrarthy, Atmakur.

Nalgonda

Huzurnagar, Nalgonda, Miryalaguda, Ramampet, Suryapet, Devarakonda.

Warangal

Mahaboobad, Farigaon, Mulug, Parkal, Narampet.

Khammam

Madhikera, Seltupalli, Yellamudu, Burgampadu, Bhadrachalam, Nugur.

Karimnagar

Peddapalli, Sirsilla, Huzurbad, Jagitial, Manthani, Adilabad, Lakethipet, Nirmal, Asifbad, Khanpur, Sirpur, Mudhole, Adilabad, Chinur, Boathutuon.

REFERENCES

1. *United Nations Organisation*, Report on the Process and Problems of Industrialisation in Underdeveloped Countries (New York) Union National, 1955) p. 16.

2. *Gunnar Myrdal*, An International Economy (New York: Harper & Brothers, 1956) p. 226.

3. *Ibid.*, p. 226.

4. *C. Ganguli*, Studies in Indian Economic Problems (Calcutta, 1978) p.1.

5. *National Institute of Small Industry* Extension Training Industrial Policy Resolution, 1980 (Hyderabad, NISIET, 1980) p. 2.

6. *Ibid.*, p. 8.

7. *Government of India*, The First Five Year Plan–A Draft outline (New Delhi: Planning Commission, 1951) p. !62.

8. *Government of India*, Second Five Year Plan (New Delhi, Planning Commission, 1956) p. 429.

9. *Government of India*, Third Five Year Plan (New Delhi, Planning Commission, 1960) p. 426.

10. *Government of India*, Fourth Five Year Plan (New Delhi: Planning Commission, 1970), p. 284.

11. *Government of India*, Draft Fifth Five Year Plan 1974-79 Volume II (New Delhi: Planning Commission, 1974) p. 160.

12. *Government of India,* Sixth Five Year Plan 1980-85 (New Delhi, Planning Commission, 1980) p. 186.

13. *State Bank of India (1988),* Seventh Five Year Plan (1985-90), Monthly Review June, p. 308.

14. *Ibid.* p. 309.

15. "Eight Plan Proposals' (1990) Economic Times Daily 31st December, pp. 1.

16. *Government of India,* Report of the Village and Small Scale Industries Committee, Second Five Year Plan, New Delhi, Planning Commission, October, 1955, p. 6.

17. *Alexander, P.C.* Industrial Estate in India", Bombay Asia Publishing House, 1963.

18. *Government of India,* Report of the Working Group on Identification of Backward Areas (Pande Working Group Report), Planning Commission.

19. *Government of India,* Report of Working Group of Fiscal and Financial Incentives for Starting Industries in Backward Areas (Report of Wanchoo Working Group: Development Commissioner, SSI, Ministry of Industrial Development).

20. *Ram, K. Vepa,* Rural Industrial Development, Development Commissioner, SSI, New Delhi, p. 246.

21. *Small Industry*—The Challenge of the Eighties, New Delhi, Vikas Publishing House Pvt. Ltd., 1983, p. 60.

22. *Sutcliffe R.B.* 'Industry and Under development 'Addisas Wesley Publishing Co. London (1971) p. 3.

23. *Barn P.A.,* Political Economy of Growth, New York (1962) p. 277.

24. *Colnean D and Ninon P, F.* Economic of Changes in Less Developed Countries, Philip Allan Publisher Ltd., Oxford (1978) p. 180.

25. UNIDO Industrial Development Strategy Reprinted in (Gerald M. Meier and edited) Leading Issues in Economic Development (3rd edition) Oxford University Press, New York (1976) p. 659.

26. *Rosenstein Radan P.N.* Problems of Industrialisation of Eastern and South Eastern Europe, Economic Journal, June-Sept. (1943).

27. Third Five Year Plan–Summary Planning Commission, Government of India, p. 47.

28. Fourth Five Year Plan, 69-74, Planning Commission, Government of India, p. 399.

29. Sixth Five Year Plan, 80-85 Planning Commission, Government of India, p. 86.

30. *Ibid.*, p. 87.

31. *Government of India*, Report of the Working Group on the Identification of Backward Areas, Planning Commission, New Delhi, 1965, p, 5.

32. *Government of India*, Fiscal and Financial Incentives for Starting Industries in Backward Areas, Development Commissioner (S.S.I.), New Delhi, 1969 p. 2-3.

33. *Government of India*, Fiscal and Financial Incentives for Starting Industries in Backward areas, Development Commissioner, (SSI), New Delhi. 1969, pp. 16-17.

34. *Government of India*, Report on Industrial Dispersal, National Committee on the Development of Backward Areas, Planning Commission, New Delhi, October, 1980, p. 12.

35. *See Appendix* for Six Points Formula and Appendix 2 for the Taluqs declined backward in different districts under six point formula.

36. *Government of A.P.,* Sixth Five Year Plan 1980-85, A.P. Department of Planning and Cooperation, Hyderabad-1980. p. 234.

37. *Government of Andhra Pradesh,* Report a Technical Committee on Identification of Backward Areas in Andhra Pradesh. Finance and Planning Department, Hyderabad 1981, pp. 2-6.

3

Socio-economic Profile of Kurnool District

(a) Location

Kurnool District lies between the Northern latitudes of 14°54' and 16°18' and the Eastern longitudes of 76°58' and 79°34'. The District of Kurnool is bounded on the north by the Thungabhadra and Krishna rivers as well as Mahaboobnagar district on the east. By Bellary district of Karnataka state on the south by Anantapur and Cuddapah districts.

There are two important mountain ranges in Kurnool district, viz., the Nallamalais and Erramalais, running parallel lines, extending from north to south. The width of the Nallamalais from the west to the east is nearly 40 kms. They lie about 113 kms. in this district extending southwards into Cuddapah district as far as the Pennar and northwards into Mahaboobnagar district beyond the Krishna. The Erramalais divide the district into two well-defined parts from east to west. The eastern part of the district lies between the Erramalais and Nallamalais comprising Nandikotkur, Nandyal, Allagadda, Koilakuntla and Banaganapalli taluks. This part of the district is crossed by the crest of the Krishna and Pennar watershed at about 1,000 meters above the sea level to the north in Nandikotkur mandal.

The Western part of the district is quite district in its features from the Eastern part of the district. The part of the district consists of Pattikonda,

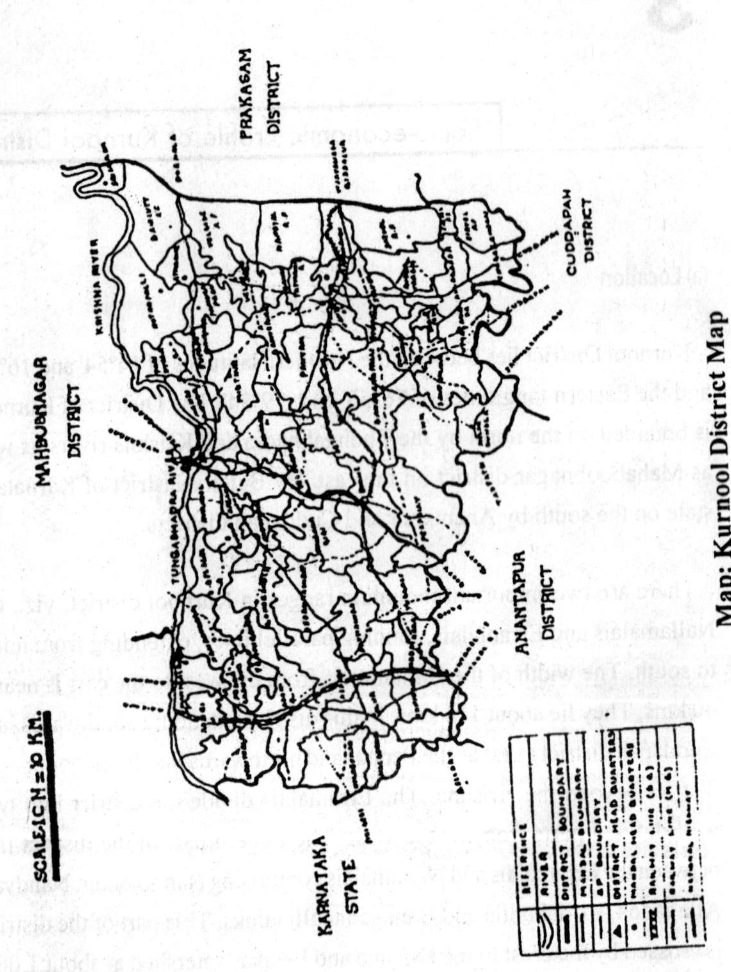

Map: Kurnool District Map

Dhone, Kurnool, Kodumur, Adoni, Yemmiganur and Alur Taluks. The ground of this part of the district, generally slopes from north to south.

This part is drained by the river Hindri, which joins the river Thungabhadra near Kurnool town.

(b) Area

Kurnool district is the third biggest district in Andhra Pradesh and is the Second biggest in Rayalaseema region with an area of 17,658 sq. kms. (at the 1991 census) which accounts for 6.42 per cent of the total area of Andhra Pradesh state (2,75,068 sq. kms.) and 26.26 per cent of total area of the Rayalaseema region of the state (67,299 sq. kms.). There are three revenue divisions viz., Kurnool, Nandyal and Adoni for administrative purpose. However, with the object of bringing administration closer to the people, 54 revenue mandals were constituted on May 25th 1985 in the place of 13 taluks in Kurnool district.

(c) Soil

Kurnool district is rich in black and red soils which constitute about 60 and 40 per cent respectively of the total soil. They are further classified as clavey, loamy and sandy soils. The black soils are predominant in the areas of Pattikonda, Nandyal, Allagadda, Koilakuntla, Nandikotkur and Adoni. In the eastern part of the district red soil of a poor quality largely predominates. These soils, although generally poor in fertility, yield a very good crop with a minimum rainfall. Regar soil of superior quality is available in the central part of the district together with Kurnool and Pattikonda areas. It responds well for paddy, indigo, bengal gram, korra, jowar and cotton in spite of alluvial soil is quite small and is confined to a few villages near Bhanavasi and Krishna rivers. It is generally suitable for raising mustard, wheat, and black gram which are valuable products.

(d) Minerals

Kurnool district possesses enormous deposits of limestone suitable for cement manufacture. It abounds in building stones of considerable variety. There are smaller deposits of iron ore, barytes, slate, steatite saline, efflorescene and quartz. The magnasite, manganese, gold and abestas occurrences in the district are only of academic interest at present. There are several occurrences of minerals of copper, lead and zinc in the district, which await detailed exploration diamonds occur in the Banaganapalli, conglomerate and aluminium at some places. Extensive deposits of lime are in Koilakuntla, Banaganapalli, Dhone, Kurnool and Nandikotkur areas, baryets in Allagadda and Nandyal.

DEMOGRAPHIC PROFILE (1991 CENSUS)

(a) Population

The district ranks eleven in population with 29.74 lakhs, people accounting for 4.48 per cent of the total population of the state, while in area it occupies the first place with 25,008 sq.kms. (about 9,218 sq. miles)

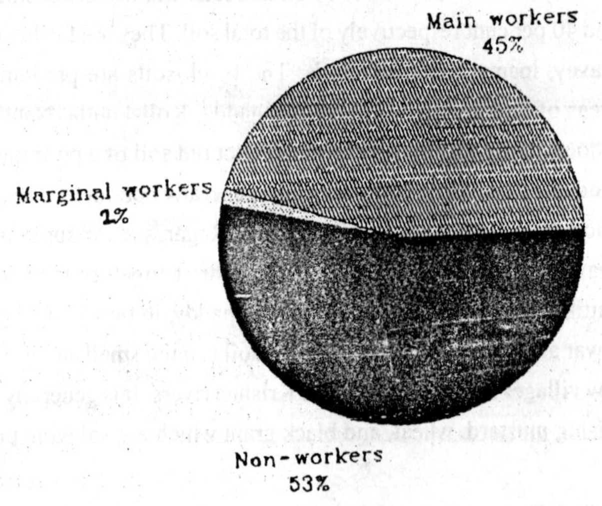

Fig.: Occupational Distribution of Population in Kurnool District

which account for 8.68 per cent of the total area of the state. (It is the largest district in the state). Kurnool district consists of 3 revenue divisions, 53 revenue mandals, 53 mandal parishads, 918 revenue villages, 4 municipalities and 821 gram panchayats.

(b) Literacy and education

The literates in the district constitute 9.67 lakhs and the literacy rate in the district as per 1991 census is 33.69 per cent. There are as many as 1819 primary schools under the management of Central Government, State Government Mandal Praja Parishad, Municipalities, aided and unaided with a student enrolment of nearly 28 lakhs and with a teachers strength of nearly 5 thousands. The number of Mandal Praja Parishad Schools accounts to 1,524 with an enrolment of nearly 22 lakhs with 3,567 teachers.

Agriculture, not only contributes the bulk of the district income, but also the main stay of the people providing livelihood for the working population.

Table 3.1
The Occupational Distribution of Population in Kurnool District.

Sl. No.	Particulars	Number	Percentage to total
1.	Main Workers	13,40,980	45.10
	(a) Cultivators	3,31,821 (24.74)	11.16
	(b) Agricultural labourers	6,64,349 (49.54)	22.35
	(c) Household Industry workers.	31.495 (2.34)	1.06
	(d) Other workers	3,13,315 (23.36)	10.54
2.	Marginal workers	41,857	1.41
3.	Non-workers	15,90,187	53.49
	Total	29,73,024	100.00

Note: Figures in brackets indicate percentage to total.
Source: Statistical Abstract of Andhra Pradesh, 1992, pp. 30-31.

The table 3.1 reveals that main workers constitute 45.10 per cent of the total population, while the non-workers constitute 53.49 per cent, marginal workers account for 1.41 per cent of the total population. Of the main workers, cultivators constitute 24.74 per cent and agricultural labourers 49.54 per cent. The remaining percentage 25.70 are house-hold industry workers (2.34) and other workers (23.36).

(a) Land Utilisation

Agriculture is the main occupation of the people of Kurnool district. About seventy per cent of the working population is engaged in agricultural sector. Food crops account for 65 per cent of the cultivated land. The pattern of the land utilisation in the district is shown in the Table 3.2.

From the table 3.2 it is clear that 52.82 per cent of the total geographical area is cultivated. Forests, barren lands, cultivable waste, grazing lands etc., put together constitute uncultivated area.

Table 3.2
Pattern of Land Utilisation

Sl. No.	Pattern of land used	Area (in Hectares)	Percentage to total geographical area
1.	Forests	3,18,250	18.08
2.	Barren and uncultivable land.	99,374	5.65
3.	Land put to Non-Agricultural uses	96,975	5.51
4.	Cultivable waste	92,540	5.26
5.	Permanent pastrues and other grazing land.	4,075	0.23
6.	Under miscellaneous tree crops not included in net area sown.	2,029	0.12
7.	Current fallows	1,80,678	10.28
8.	Other fallow lands	1,30,198	7.40
9.	Net area sown	8,35,915	47.49
	Total geographical area	17,60,034	100.00

Source: Government of Andhra Pradesh, Statistical Abstract, 1992, pp. 80-81.

(b) Source of irrigation

The Irrigation facilities available in Kurnool district are meagre as it is evident from the fact that only about 12.80 per cent of the net sown area was irrigated during the year 1986-88, as against 35.33 per cent for the state as a whole. The important sources of irrigation in the district are canals, tanks and wells. The canals worth mentioning are K.C. Canal, Thungabhadra Project Low level Canal, Thungabhadra Project High level Canal, Zerreru Project and Gazuladinne Project. The total irrigated area is about 134 thousand hectares. This formed about 15.14 per cent of the gross area sown in the district. Canals are principal sources of irrigation covering 71-03 per cent of the total net irrigated area in the district. Wells are the next important source of irrigation covering 17.76 per cent of the total net irrigated area. The area irrigated by tanks is 6.54 per cent. The area irrigated by other sources if lowest in the district at 4.67 per cent of the total net irrigated.

(c) Size of land holdings

Size of land holdings in Kurnool district is shown in the Table 3.3.

Table 3.3
Size of Land Holdings in Kurnool District

Size class of holding	Percentage distribution of holdings	Percentage land holdings operated.
Below 1.0	32.95	5.68
1.0 to 2.0	23.39	10.68
2.0 to 4.0	21.73	18.12
4.0 to 10.0	16.14	31.51
10.0 to above	5.79	34.01
Total	100.00	100.00

Source: Government of Andhra Pradesh Statistical Abstract 1992. pp. 122-123.

Nearly one-third of total land-holdings are below one hectare. Further, about one fifth of land holdings are in the category of 1 to 2 hectares. Though about 55 per cent of total land holdings are below 2 hectares, not all of them are operated. Perhaps the owners of small holdings may not have the requisite resources to convert their farms into viable units. Understandably, the percentage of land holdings operated is higher in the category of ten hectares and above.

(d) Cropping Pattern

Jowar, Korra and rice are the principal food crops. Cotton and Groundnuts are the cash crops grown in the district. The details of the cropping pattern for the year 1986-87 indicates that jowar occupies the largest portion of the total cropped area (25.48) followed by groundnut (21.41), Korra (15.43), rice (7.06), Cotton (4.48) and bazra (3.50). As much as 77.40 per cent of the total cropped area is covered by these crops together. The total net cropped area in the district is 836 thousand hectares. Out of this total cropped area, the total food crops and the total non-food crops accounted for 57.54 per cent and 42.46 per cent respectively.

The productivity of principal crops in the district in terms of kgs. per hectare is as follows. Rice 2,159, groundnut 702, jowar 554, bazra 368 and korra 337. It is obvious that the productivity of all the principal crops was very low, mainly due to low and erratic rainfall, resulting in soil moisture deficiency low fertility of soils, traditional methods of farming and other factors.

(e) Rural labour force in Kurnool district

According to 1991 census, the population of Kurnool district was 29,73,024 and out of it 13,82,837 people were workers. The agricultural labour force in Kurnool district as per 1991 census was 6,64,349. Total workers accounted for 46.51 per cent in the total population of the district.

SOCIAL INFRASTRUCTURE

(a) Schools

Literacy is the ability of a person to read and write and communicate with the outside world where as education is the systematic instruction, schooling or training given to young persons in preparation for the work of life. The facilities available for the education of the people in the district is shown in Table 3.4 (page 82).

From the Table 3.4 it is clear that there is one school for every 186 students and one teacher for every 48 students.

(b) Hospitals

The district has got one general hospital at the headquarters. There are 15 hospitals, 89 dispensaries and one hospital for special treatment, with 429 government doctors. The total beds strength is 1,481 and it work out to one bed per 1,626 persons.

ECONOMIC INFRA STRUCTURE

(a) Transport and Communication

The most important railway line in the district is the North-West mainline of the Southern railway connecting Madras in the south and Bombay in west. All important towns and villages in the district are well-connected by a net-work of roads. On an average 90 per cent of the villages have road facilities. Some are connected by pucca road remaining by kuccha roads.

The district has 2,209 km. length of roads under P.W.D. and R & B. The roads maintained by Zilla Praja Parishad accounts for a length of 1,464.45 kms. Panchayat Samithi roads accounts for a length of 2,000 kms. On the road the district has 5,084 vehicles constituting 424 are APSRTC, 72 are

Table 3.4
Type of Schools in Kurnool District

Sl.No.	Type of School	Number	Students			Teachers		
			Boys	Girls	Total	Men	Women	Total
1.	Primary Schools	1,735	1,57,506	1,04,912	2,62,418	2,858	1,347	4,205
2.	Upper Primary Schools	155	32,964	18,591	51,555	731	412	1,143
3.	High Schools	189	52,153	21,148	73,301	2,285	500	2,785
Total		2,079	2,42,623	1,54,651	3,87,274	5,874	2,259	8,133

Source: Government of Andhra Pradesh, Statistical Abstract, 1992, pp. 70-71.

private buses, 972 public lorries, 62 contract carriages, 900 cars and jeeps, 52 tractors, 504 tractors trailers, 2,883 motor cycles and scooters and the rest are ordinary trailers etc. In Kurnool district there are 5 Head Post Offices, 136 sub-offices, 49 telephone exchanges and 4,286 phones. The length of broad guage railway track is 95 km. and of meter guage is 151 km.

A substantial proportion of the heavy and voluminous traffic into and outside the district is moved by the railways. The buses are contributed largely to the development of rural and urban areas.

(b) Banking

There are 168 bank branches in the district under 20 bank organisations. Among them 91 are regional rural banks, 38 urban banks and 39 are semi-urban banks. The Syndicate Bank is the Lead Bank in the district. The population served per bank branch office works out to 14,000. The Andhra Pradesh State Financial Corporation has a branch office at Kurnool.

INDUSTRIAL PROFILE

In the Rayalaseema region, Kurnool district has a fairly larger units in large-scale sector. These units are mostly agro-based. A detailed picture of industries and their organisation in the district is presented in Table 3.5.

Table 3.5
Industries in Kurnool District

Item		Number
Number of Factories		338
All workers		14,528
All employees		17,668
Fixed capital	(Rupees in lakhs)	6,994
Working capital	"	2,286
Productive capital	"	9,290
Wages to workers	"	968
Total emoluments	"	1,421
Total input	"	16,071
Total output	"	19,701
Depreciation	"	770
Value added	"	2,859

Source: Government of Andhra Pradesh, Statistical Abstract, 1992 (Hyderabad: Bureau of Economics and Statistics, 1992), pp. 166-167.

4

Industrial Development in Kurnool District

Kurnool is regarded as an industrially backward district. The rate of industrial development is relatively low. Though several measures have been initiated to accelerate industrial development in the district. These include offering investment subsidies, providing industrial infrastructure, extending vocational training support and offering concessional finances, especially for the small and tiny units.

The existing industrial scene in the district is dotted by the presence of a relatively small number of Large and Medium Scale units, a fairly large number of Registered Small Scale Units and a very large number of unregistered Non-farm Sector Units.

Large and Medium Scale Units

There are, presently 25 large and medium scale units in the district with an estimated aggregate capital investment of Rs. 435 Crores and employing over 10,000 persons.

A list of the Large and Medium Scale units set up in the district as given in vide Annexure—III.

Activity-wise distribution of these units, points to the predominance of chemical and agro base units, followed by textile, food and mineral base units, as detailed below.

Activity-wise Distribution of Large and Medium Scale Units in Kurnool District

S.No.	Category	Units	Investment Rs. Crores	Employment Nos.
1.	Chemical	5	206.36	598
2.	Agro	4	130.04	781
3.	Textile	3	12.90	2,477
4.	Mineral	2	36.88	910
5.	Food	4	15.15	2,023
	Total	18	401.33	6,789

Note: Sick units Omitted.

The chemical base units are engaged in the manufacture of a wide variety of basic chemicals as caustic soda, liquid chlorine, hydrochloric acid, staple bleaching powder, high strength hypo chlorite, calcium carbide, oxygen, and LPG bottling.

The agro base units relate to edible oil extraction and refining, writing and printing paper, and crystal sugar manufacturing.

While the textile base units are engaged in the manufacture of cotton yarn, the mineral base units are engaged mainly in the manufacture of portland cement. The food base units are engaged in diverse activities as vanaspati manufacturing, processing of liquid milk and soft drinks bottling.

It is however important to note that as a majority of the large and medium units in the district are continuous processing units, their contribution for the development of the small scale ancillaries seems to be low.

The geographical spread of these units points to locational concentration in and around Kurnool, Adoni, Nandyal and Yemmiganur towns. Further, the locational choice seems to have been guided more by proximity to raw material sources.

Field level discussions indicate that only 50% of the large and medium units are functioning well, the remaining, while a majority are limping, the rest were declared as sick units and ceased functioning.

Small Scale Units

As at March, 1997, there are 3,989 registered small scale units in the district with an estimated aggregate investment of Rs. 64.45 crores and providing employment to 22,870 persons.

Activity-wise distribution of these units reveals the predominance of mineral base units followed agro, forest, engineering, chemical and food base units.

The Activity-wise distribution of SSI units in Kurnool district is as follows:

S.No.	Activity	Units	Investment Rs. Lakhs	Employment Nos.
1.	Agro Based	754	1,605.14	4,735
2.	Mineral Based	1,035	1,542,97	7,130
3.	Food Based	120	69.84	772
4.	Chemical Based	188	831.08	1,804
5.	Engg. Based	576	508.63	2,435
6.	Leather Based	45	15.05	195
7.	Textile Based	25	30.85	153
8.	Forest Based	137	116.82	1,288
9.	Miscellaneous	929	612.57	3,124
	Total	3,989	6,444.95	22,870

Cuddapah Slab polishing units, Rice Shellers, Dal Mills, Groundnut Decorticators, Oil Expellers and rotaries predominate the small industry scene in the district.

Other important lines of activity include PVC pipes manufacturing, roller flour milling, manufacture of instant foods, pharmaceuticals, detergents, readymade garments, bricks, paper cones, warping and sizing of yarn, pulverising of minerals, charcoal manufacturing, wooden furniture and joinery, general engineering workshops, footwear manufacturing etc.

The geographical distribution of the SSI units in the district reveals a relative concentration of these units in the Mandals of Nandyal, Kurnool, Adoni, Dhone, Kallur, Bethamcharla, Kolinigundla, Atmakurand Yemmiganur.

While the overall performance of the SSI units in the district is reportedly satisfactory, these are 40 sick SSI units distributed over a cross-section of manufacturing activities.

Unregistered Tiny Units

In addition to the registered small and tiny units, there are a sizably large number of unregistered tiny units engaged in handloom weaving, and a myriad manufacturing/processing, servicing and trading activities. No reliable data are available as to the number of such units, investments made in them, employment generated, business turnovers etc.

The unregistered tiny units however make a significant contribution to the district economy, especially from the view point of providing lasting self-employment avenues to artisans and; educated unemployed.

Government Initiatives for Self-employment Promotion

Several Policy measures have been initiated for the promotion of self-employment and entrepreneurship among different target groups through the establishment of specific institutions and lanching of several schemes. Mention could be made in this regard of measures such as extending margin money support, investment subsidy composite loans and concessional finances.

Among the institutions catering to the growth of small business and entrepreneurship are the District Industries Centre (DIC), Scheduled Caste Cooperative Finance Corporation, Backward Classes Cooperative Finance Corporation, District Rural Development Agency (DRDA), and AP minorities Finance Corporation (APMFC), and Commissionerate of Youth Services.

The number of beneficiaries assisted by these Institutions and the type of employment opportunities propagated in the district are discussed below:

Prime Minister's Rojgar Yojana (PMRY)

PMRY, a Central Government sponsored programme aims at promotions of self-employment and entrepreneurship among educated unemployed youth primarily through imparting entrepreneurial training and extension of financial assistance upto Rs. 1.00 lakh per beneficiary to help set up tiny manufacturing, servicing and trading venture.

A total of 2431 beneficiaries were extended support in Kurnool District, under PMRY during 1993-94 to 1996-97 (details vide Annexure—IV).

Chief Minister's Empowerment of Youth (CMEY) Programme

CMEY was launched during 1996-97 to help rural youth to form into cohesive groups and take to viable economic activities. During 1996-97, a total 391 youth groups were formed in the district and tiny units established to undertake a wide range of group economic activities (details vide Annexure—V)

Assistance by SC Corporation

Scheduled Caste Cooperative Finance Corporation also has been extending financial assistance through provision of margin money and term loans from NSFDC to potential entrepreneurs belonging to Scheduled Castes. During 1994-95 and 1996-97, more than 2000 beneficiaries were extended financial assistance in the district to enable them to set up self-employment ventures (details vide Annexure—VI).

Assistance by BC Corporation

Andhra Pradesh Backward Classes Cooperative Finance Corporation has been extending financial assistance to potential entrepreneurs among Backward Classes through provision of margin money and term loan under NBCFDC. During 1994-95 to 1996-97, nearly 1800 beneficiaries availed assistance to set up their small self-employment ventures (details vide Annexure—VII).

The promotional measures initiated thus far have made a positive impact on the promotion of self-employment in the district. Nevertheless, the existing pattern of opportunity preference by beneficiary shows an excessive degree of preference towards conventional and business activities. It would be imperative to promote more of manufacturing and servicing activities.

Ancillaries

Development of small scale ancillary units to cater to the industrial needs of large and medium scale industries is an important aspect of small development in the country.

There are 25 large and medium scale industrial units in Kurnool District engaged in product groups such as basic chemicals, writing paper, oil refining, sugar, portland cement, prestressed concrete sleepers, soft drinks, cotton yarn etc.

Notwithstanding the presence of the large and medium scale units, development of ancillaries in the district has been low and tardy. As at March, 1997 there are only two ancillary units catering to the industrial requirements of M/s. Sree Rayalaseema Alkalies and Allied Chemicals Ltd., and M/s. ITC Agro Tech. Ltd. The ancillary unit to the former manufacturers barium sulphate and barium carbonate, while that to the latter manufacturers plastic and tin containers of different sizes.

The major factors attributed to the low development ancillaries in the district are:

i) A majority of the mother units are continuous process units and hence the potential for ancillary development is generally low.
ii) Some of the major mother units, are those engaged in the manufacture of writing paper, vanaspati, cotton yarn have either become sick or have been functioning marginally resulting in low development of ancillaries.
iii) In the present day context, the mother units believe in depending more on enlisted vendors and small scale suppliers for a large number of products rather than promoting exclusive ancillaries.

LARGE AND MEDIUM SCALE INDUSTRIES UNDER IMPLEMENTATION

Sl.No.	Name of the Industry	Mandal	Activity	Latest Stage
1.	Sri Vishnupriya Industries Ltd.	Panyam	C.R. Rolled Sheets	Under Progress
2.	Sri Rayalaseema Hi-Strength Hypo Ltd.	Kurnool	Trichloro Acetic Acid	Land acquired, Arranged finance
3.	Sri Rayalaseema Alkalies and Allied Chem. Ltd.	Kurnool	Vanaspathi	Land & Power acquired
4.	Ragsan Petrochem. Ltd.	Kallur	LPG Bottling	Lr. addressed. Awaiting Production Shorty
5.	Sree Rayalaseema Alkalies and Allied Chem. Ltd.	Kurnool	Distilled fatty acid	Likely to go into Commercial Production shortly
6.	Sree Rayalaseema Hi-Strength Hypo. Ltd.	Kurnool	Sulphur Dioxide Lqd.	Expecting production shortly
7.	Sree Rayalaseema Alkalies and Allied Chem. Ltd.	Kurnool	Mineral fibre	Land, Power, Finance acquired
8.	Sree Rayalaseema Alkalies and Allied Chem. Ltd.	Kurnool	Undelcylanic Acid	Likely to go into production shortly
9.	Sree Rayalaseema Alkalies and Allied Chem. Ltd.	Kurnool	N-N-Bisamide	Expected to go into production shortly
10.	Sree Rayalaseema Alkalies and Allied Chem. Ltd.	Kurnool	Heptal Dehyce	Expected to go into production shortly
11.	Sree Rayalaseema Alkalies and Allied Chem. Ltd.	Kurnool	Para Bisamide	Expected to go into production shortly
12.	Sree Rayalaseema Alkalies and Allied Chem. Ltd.	Kurnool	Dehydrated Castor Oil	Expected to go into production shortly
13.	Sree Rayalaseema Hi-Strength Hypo. Ltd.	Kurnool	Calcium Sulphate	Expected to go into production shortly
14.	Nu. Tech Crganic Chemicals Ltd.	Adoni	Acid Oils	Awaiting approvals
15.	Nu-Tech Organic Chemicals Ltd.	Adoni	Distilled Fatty AcID	Awaiting approvals
16.	Sree Rayalaseema Hi-Strength Hypo Ltd.	Kurnool	Ncn-Farric Alum	Likely to go into production shortly
17.	Sree Rayalaseema Alkalies and Allied Chem. Ltd.	Kurnool	Bleach liquor	Likely to go into production shortly
18.	Sree Rayalaseema Alkalies and Allied Chem. Ltd.	Kurnool	Fatty acids	Expected to go into production shortly
19	Sree Rayalaseema Alkalies and Allied Chem. Ltd.	Kurnool	Melayl 12-hydroxy stearate	Expected to go into production shortly

LARGE AND MEDIUM SCALE INDUSTRIES WITH AN INVESTMENT OF ABOVE RS. 25.00 CRORES

Sl.No.	Name of the Industry	Mandal	Activity	Latest Stage
1.	Sri Vijaya Lakshmi Industries Ltd..	Koilakuntla	Ordinary Portland Cement	Prospective licence obtained. Awaiting for mining
2.	Sri Vishnupriya Industris Ltd.	Panyam	Flat Rolled products of Iron or Non alloy steel	
3.	Sri Vishnupriya Industris Ltd.	Panyam	Flat Rolled products of Iron at	Under Planning
4.	Prism Cement Ltd.	Kolimigundla	Portland cement	Awaiting environmental clearance.

S.No.	Year category	1997-1998			1998-99			1999-2000		
		No	Inv.	Emp.	No	Inv.	Emp.	No.	Inv.	Emp.
1.	Agro Based	180	198	900	186	213.9	930	193	231.6	1158
2.	Mineral Based	155	341	1085	160	352	1120	166	365.2	1162
3.	Engg. Based	135	108	675	139	118.15	695	144	122.4	720
4.	Chemical Based	30	78	240	31	80.60	248	32	84.8	256
5.	Textile Based	60	33	300	62	37.20	372	65	42.25	325
6.	Forest Based	55	60.5	275	57	62.70	285	59	73.75	295
7.	Miscellaneous	185	222	905	191	229.20	1060	198	267.30	1290
8.	SSSBE	120	66	240	124	74.40	372	128	102.40	384
	Total	920	1106.50	4620	950	1168.15	5082	985	1289.70	5590

INV : Investment Rs in Lakhs, *EMP*: Employment Generation, *No*: Number of Units.

5

Conclusion

Industrialisation has a major role to play in economic development in the developing countries like India. The most pressing need of many developing countries of the world today is rapid industrialisation for achieving basic objectives of their economic and social progress and for raising the living standards of the people. The process of industrialisation involves those basic changes which raise productivity of factors which would result in high average income.

Industrialisation also helps in increasing prosperity of a country and provides employment for skilled semi-skilled unskilled labour. The Government of India has been encouraging heavy industries only in the field where they are absolutely necessary. Development of Small Scale Industries is a happy blend of automation and primitive ways of production.

The role of village and small-scale industries in the development of national economy has been stressed by the Government of India in its Industrial Policy Resolution of 1956 and in the successive Five Year Plan documents. The main advantage of small-scale industries is that they provide large scale employment at relatively smaller capital cost. Small Industries are expected to meet a substantial part of the increased demand for consumer goods and simple producers goods. They facilitate mobilisation of resources and skill which might otherwise remain unutilised.

Economic Development of a country depends upon the utility of its people to use new techniques which ensure high production industry not only produces the inputs required for the introduction of modern science and technology but it also helps to produce an army of people with technicians, accountants, economists and so on, who help to use these inputs with dynamic effects on economic development.

There is a positive relationship between industrialisation and economic development. In countries like India and Japan with a high ratio of population to natural resources and in particulars to land, manufacturing industry represents virtually the only hope of greatest increasing labour products and raising levels of living.

It would be appropriate for an under developing country to concentrate investible resources initially on the development of agriculture sector and other simple industrial activities which do not absorb much capital.

SMALL SCALE INDUSTRIES IN INDIA, POLICIES, PROGRAMMES AND PERFORMANCE

The small scale industries have enough scope to exploit available local resources such as small savings, raw materials, skilled and unskilled labour. Further, they generate income for consumption of wage goods and provide employment to unemployed persons. So, it is necessary to allot public sector investment for development of infrastructural facilities and provide incentive through developmental programmes for setting up of small industries.

The Industrial Policy Resolution (1948) stressed the need for development of small scale industries. The objectives of the policy are:

(1) To establish a social order where justice and equality of opportunities could be assured

(2) To raise the standard of living of the people through exploitation of talents and available resources of the country.

(3) To accelerate production to meet the needs of the growing population and

(4) To provide more and opportunities for employment. This policy was in force up to 1956.

During the First Five Year Plan, a major steps taken for development of village and small industries was the establishment of small scale industries boards to advise and assist the Central Government in the formation of programmes for development of handloom industry, khadi and village industries, small scale industries, handicrafts, sericulture and coir, International Team of experts was invited by the Government of India in 1953 to study the problems of small scale industries. The team recommended the establishment of Regional Small Industries Service Institute and accordingly four such Institutes were set up at Bombay, Calcutta, Madurai and Faridabad with branch units, in Uttar Pradesh, Bihar, Andhra Pradesh and Travancore-Cochin. These Institutes provide various kinds of technical services to village and small industries, such as information about improved techniques of production, technical advise and assistance in the utilisation of the local raw materials". The programme of work of the small scale Industries Board follows largely the lines indicated in the Report of the International Planning Team. The main part of the programme was the establishment of a number of Institutes for organisation, technical servicing and business connecting and marketing assistance.

The Industrial Estates programme was started in 1955 following the recommendations of the International Planning Team. Under this programme, suitable sites with all the facilities such as water, electricity, transport, steam, communications, Banks, Post-office, raw materials depots, canteens, watch and ward, First-Aid etc., are to be provide so as to create the necessary climate for the development of small industries. The main objectives of the industrial estates programme are:

1. To shift the Small Scale Industries from congested areas to industrial estates with a view to increasing this productivity.
2. To achieve decentralised industrial development in small town and villages and,
3. To assist ancillary industries in the townships surrounding major industrial undertakings, both in the public and private sector. The Government of India had given a big boost under different Five Year Plans by encouraging the establishment of Industrial Estates in the country.

PRESENT STUDY

Area-specific micro level studies will be useful to know the development of small scale industries pertaining to different regions in the country, particularly backward region. Against this background, the present study is attempted covering Kurnool District of Andhra Pradesh.

Agriculture is the main occupation of the people of Kurnool District as about 70 per cent of the working population depends on agriculture, either directly or indirectly.

The District Industries Centre was started in 1978 for the promotion of small scale, tiny village and cottage industries. There has been a steady increase in small scale industries.

Bibliography

BOOKS

1. Alexander, P.C., *Industrial Estates in India,* Asia Publishing House, 1963.

2. Bandyopadhyaya, K., *Industrialisation through Industrial Estates,* Bookland, Private Limited, Calcutta, 1969.

3. Basu, S.K., *Place and Problems of Small Scale Industries,* A. Mukharjee & Company (P) Ltd., Calcutta, 1957.

4. Bharti, R.K., *Industrial Estates in Developing Economics*, National Publishing House, Delhi, 1978.

5. Bredo, William, *Industrial Estates, Tool for Industrialisation, Stanford Research Institute*, California, 1960.

6. Deepak Agrawal, *Prospects of Industrial Estates in Underdeveloped Countries,* Chugh Publications, Allahabad, 1987.

7. Dhar, P.N. and Lydall, H.F., *The Role of Small Enterprises in Indian Economic Development*, Delhi Institute of Economic Growth, 1961.

8. Gadgil, D. R., *The Industrial Evolution of India in recent times,* Oxford University Press, London, 1959.

9. Joshi, Naveen, C., *Cottage and Small Scale Industry in India,* Suneja Book Centre, New Delhi 1956.

10. Jyothi Rani T., *Sickness in Small Scale Industrial Sector*, Sandeep Publishing House, Warangal, 1985.

11. Lakdawala and Sandesara, *Small Industry in a Big City*, University of Bombay, Publication Bombay, 1961.

12. Mathur, O.P., *Manual on Industrial Estates Plans,* SIET Institute Hyderabad, 1971.

13. Myrdal, Gunnar, *Economic Theory and Underdevelopment Regions*, Gerald Duckworth and Company London, 1957.

14. Nagaiya, D., *Industrial Estates Programme. The Indian Experience*, SIET Institute, Hyderabad, 1971.

15. Nanjundan, S. Robinson, H.E., and Staley, Eugene, *Economic Research for Small Industry Development*, Stanford Research Institute, California, 1960.

16. Ramkrishna, K.T., *Finances for Small Scale Industry in India*, Asia Publishing House, Bombay, 1963.

17. Rao, R.V., *Small Industries and the Developing Economy in India*, Concept Publishing House, New Delhi, 1979.

18. Rao, V.K.R.V., *Role of Small Scale Enterprises in India Economic Development*, Asia Publishing House, Bombay, 1961.

19. Ruddar Dutt and Sundaram, K.P.M., *Indian Economy,* S. Chand and Company Limited, New Delhi, 1990.

20. Sarma, Ramkrishna, *Industrial Development of Andhra Pradesh*, Himalaya Publishing House, 1982.

21. Satyanarayana, *Industrial Development in Backward Regions, Resources and Planning*, Chugh Publications, Allahabad, 1989.

22. Singh, Baljit, *The Economics of Small Scale Industries*, A case study of small scale establishments of Moradabad, Asia Publishing House, Bombay, 1961.

23. Somasekhara, N., *The Efficacy of Industrial Estates in India*, Vikas Publishing House, New Delhi, 1975.

24. Srinivasan, *Industrial Estates Management*, Maruthi Book Depot Guntur, 1981.

25. Subbi Reddy, T., *Industrial Estates in India Vora and Company*, Bombay, 1970.

26. Vakil, C.N., *Industrial Development in India* (Policies and Problems), Orient Longmans, 1973.

27. Vasant, Desai, *Organisation and Management of Small Scale Industries*, Himalaya Publishing House, 1983.

28. Vepa K. Ram., *Industrial Development in Andhra Pradesh*, M. Seshachalam and Company, Machilipatnam, 1968.

29. Vepa K. Ram, *Small Industries in Japan*, Vora and Company, Bombay, 1967.

30. Vepa K. Ram, *Small Industry in the Seventies*, Vikas Publishing House, New Delhi, 1971.

REPORTS

1. Development Commissioner Small Scale Industries Government of India, New Delhi. — Report on Industrial Estates in India, New Delhi, 1967.

2. District Industries Centre, Anantapur. — Annual Report from 1987-90.

3. Government of Andhra Pradesh, Andhra Pradesh Industrial Infrastructure Corporation Limited (APIIC) — 1 Annual Reports from 1980-90. 2. Note on activities of the APIIC, 1990.

4. Government of India Planning Commission. — First Five Year Plan, 1951. Second Five Year Plan, 1956. Third Five Year Plan, 1961. Fourth Five Year Plan, 1969. Fifth Five Year Plan, 1974. Sixth Five Year Plan, 1980. Seventh Five Year Plan, 1985.

United Nations Reports

1. Establishment of Industrial Estates in Developing Countries, 1978.

2. The Effectiveness of Industrial Estates in Developing Countries, 1978.

Index